Five Frequencies

Leadership Signals that turn Culture into Competitive Advantage

Jeff Grimshaw | Tanya Mann
Lynne Viscio | Jennifer Landis

Publisher: Helio Fred Garcia

Editor: Holly Helstrom

Copyright © 2019 Jeff Grimshaw | Tanya Mann

Lynne Viscio | Jennifer Landis

All rights reserved. ISBN-13: 978-1097432059

ISBN-10: 1097432059

Logos Institute Best Practices Series

Logos Institute for Crisis Management and Executive Leadership Press

Logos Institute Best Practices Series

The Logos Institute for Crisis Management and Executive Leadership stands at the intersection of scholarship and practice, providing both rigorous analysis and practical application of key leadership principles. We illuminate best practices, current trends, emerging issues, and leadership skills.

The Logos Institute is a thought leader in its field, conducting research, publishing, and providing an extensive range of executive education workshops, seminars, conferences, and highly-customized coaching for senior executives of all sectors and around the world.

The Logos Institute creates and maintains an inventory of Best Practices, along with attendant tools and concepts that can inform our clients of what works and why, and that can help our clients to enhance their capacity to perform at higher and higher levels. We harness and publish these best practices in a number of ways, from full-length books published by major publishing houses to chapters of or forewords to books, to articles in peer-reviewed scholarly and management journals, to contributions to mainstream media, social media, and blogs. We also publish highly distilled checklists on dozens of high-stakes decision-making, communication, or crisis-related situations.

The *Logos Institute Best Practices Series* provides conceptual frame works that help to make sense of complicated issues, combined with case studies, examples, and actionable tools, tips, and techniques that help leaders make smart choices and build competitive advantage in high-stakes situations.

CONTENTS

ACKNOWLEDGMENTS

We're grateful to many, including Helio Fred Garcia and Holly Helstrom at Logos. Also: David Spach, Scott Bolger, Domenic Christopher, Shawn Patterson, Sarah Voeffray, Kara Lynn Noto, Mary Messana, Rob Nissen, Bob Sturmer, Sydney Zack, MaryAnne Casha, Ed Kokosky, Debra Pospiech, Dr. Debra Silberg, Aaron Eu-Wei Yeo, Nancy Marcucci, Keith Polson, Dean Edwards, Steve Fine, Laura Hughes, Janet Lindner, and Amy Goldfinger. Thank you to LiamDesigns for the cover and frequency art. We're also grateful to Charlotte Grimshaw for proofreading. Finally, much love to the Grimshaw, Landis, Mann, and Wilkie-Viscio families for their input, support, and encouragement.

Some of the concepts and examples in this book previously appeared in *Leadership without Excuses: How to Create Accountability and High Performance (Instead of Just Talking about It)*, by Jeff Grimshaw and Gregg Baron, published by McGraw-Hill (2010).

Five Frequencies® and Know / Feel / Do® are registered trademarks of MGStrategy.

FOREWORD

I met Jeff Grimshaw in 2003, almost by accident. I was then a crisis advisor to a large insurance company that, at the time, was persistently in trouble. I had spent a full year on site at the company in the year 2000 and by 2003 I was there about half the time. I had given lots of advice, and some of it had been implemented. But it was a struggle sometimes for the advice to go up the chain or across the organization.

One day I walked into a meeting and found myself sitting across from someone who was introduced only as Jeff. Turns out that he had been advising the same company for about the same amount of time on the same issues. I later learned that his focus was mostly internal culture and employee communication, while mine was crisis management in general. But I had no idea who he was. So, as sometimes happens, we two consultants circled each other warily throughout the meeting, wondering, "Who is this invader messing with my relationship with my client?"

But as it happens, we ended up giving the client the same advice. We each phrased it a bit differently, but it was the same. We got to speaking afterward, and discovered we had similar approaches to client work. Not identical, but aligned. And a great and productive relationship and friendship began. We started by presenting jointly to that client. And the client began taking our collective advice, which got through the organization more effectively than before.

We have since worked with other mutual clients, and have referred each other to prospective clients. I have had Jeff speak in my New York University communication strategy course. Jeff and Tanya Mann authored the employee engagement chapter of the second edition of *Reputation Management: The Key to Successful Public Relations and Corporate Communication*, which I co-authored with John Doorley. Jeff, Tanya, and Lynne Viscio co-authored that chapter in the third edition. And I made a small contribution to Jeff's and Gregg Baron's outstanding book, *Leadership Without Excuses: How to Create Accountability and High Performance (Instead of Just Talking About It)*.

I know Jeff, Tanya, Lynne, and Jennifer Landis to be inspired and inspiring strategists, counselors, and communicators. And *Five Frequencies* is a remarkable book in many ways. First, it makes sense. Second, it's accessible. And third, it packs great insight into an easy-to-follow framework. Take it seriously and you will be able to build competitive advantage by bridging the gap between the culture you have and the culture you need.

As the publisher of the Logos Institute for Crisis Management and Executive Leadership Press, I could not be happier that our first book by a non-Logos author is *Five Frequencies*.

Helio Fred Garcia
New York City, May, 2019

INTRODUCTION

Your organization's culture: It's either an asset or a liability. At this very moment, your culture is helping business performance. Or hurting it. (The latter is what management guru Peter Drucker meant when he said, "culture eats strategy for breakfast.")

There's another relevant Drucker quote: "You can't manage what you don't measure."

That's why we do what we do: We help leaders measure and manage culture. Specifically, we help them establish a reliable culture metric, measure the gap between *the culture they have* and *the culture they need*, and then close it.

And when leaders measurably strengthen culture, business performance follows.

How do you measurably strengthen culture? How do you turn culture into competitive advantage? Based on 20 years of research, the answer couldn't be clearer: Intentionally or unintentionally, leaders create culture through the signals they broadcast on Five Frequencies®:

1. Their decisions and actions
2. What they reward and recognize
3. What they tolerate (or don't)

4. How they show up informally

5. Their formal communications

To measurably strengthen culture, you've got to be intentional. To make a bad culture good, or a good culture great, you've got to deliberately transmit strong and steady signals across all Five Frequencies.

Even if this intuitively makes sense, you probably want examples.

Sadly, sometimes it's easier to find bad examples than good ones. Going back a few years, Enron is the classic example of what not to do.

- They won awards for their slick formal communications (Frequency 5). These included videos in which their CEO Ken Lay, and COO Jeff Skilling touted the company's commitment to a culture of respect and integrity.

- But those values were not what Lay and Skilling exemplified in their decisions and actions (Frequency 1). For example, they used accounting tricks to hide mountains of debt and toxic assets. That's no way to show integrity or respect to investors and creditors.

- Respect and integrity were also not what they rewarded (Frequency 2). Instead, they rewarded aggressive, risk-taking behavior and basically anything, no matter how questionable, as long as it helped the company meet quarterly earnings targets. ("We were a hurdle, a speed bump, but not an obstacle," said a former Managing Director of the group that was supposed to manage risk.)[1]

- The Enron culture that ultimately destroyed itself was also a function of what Lay, Skilling, and other leaders tolerated (Frequency 3). For example, executives and employees frequently entertained clients and bankers at strip clubs in the middle of the workday, billing the cost back to their Enron expense accounts.

- How leaders showed up informally (Frequency 4) also contributed to Enron's demise. Many top managers lacked the ability and willingness to manage and engage their staff. They said they preferred a "hands off" style, but what it meant was that internal controls were weak. Other leaders sent culture-shaping signals on Frequency 4 with their frequent in-office temper tantrums.

You may remember how this story ended: Bankruptcy, jail time, 20,000 hardworking employees losing jobs and health insurance, and the evaporation of $2 billion in pensions.

A more recent example of bad culture eventually catching up with performance is Wells Fargo. A 2017 Barron's survey found they are now the least respected company in America, right behind Big Tobacco's Philip Morris.[2] How did this banking institution, once exalted in Jim Collins' *Good to Great*, go bad? Like anywhere else, leaders shaped culture with the signals they broadcast on Five Frequencies:

- Just like Enron, Wells Fargo had great formal communications (Frequency 5). Full (and sheepish) disclosure: A few years back we touted their formal communication prowess in a graduate school textbook, Reputation Management, to which we contributed a chapter. What we liked was how Wells Fargo used artful and consistent communication to help employees see how their work enabled customers to pursue the American Dream.

- But it turned out that while those customers were dreaming, Wells Fargo's senior leaders' decisions and actions (Frequency 1) enabled fraud. The executive team's decision to try to sell every customer eight products (because eight rhymes with great, they noted) translated into the company opening—and collecting fees on—more than two million unauthorized customer accounts.[3]

- Perhaps what damaged the culture most is what they rewarded (Frequency 2). Warren Buffett, whose Berkshire owns a $25 billion stake in Wells Fargo, rebuked its leaders when he discovered they'd "incentivized the wrong type of behavior."[4] They did that by setting ridiculously aggressive sales goals, rewarding those who found a way to meet them (even when it meant cheating), and hounding, and in many cases, terminating those who didn't.

- What they tolerated (Frequency 3) was the cheating they'd incentivized. The company's Code of Ethics claimed that "gaming" (the manipulation and / or misrepresentation of sales or referrals) was against the rules and grounds for dismissal. But for more than ten years, anyone who called attention to the blatant gaming was either ignored or actively silenced. According to one former employee, "Management made it clear that no employee was allowed to complain about the unethical practices that were going on within the branch."[5]

- How CEO John Stumpf showed up informally (Frequency 4) also shaped the culture and contributed to Wells Fargo's troubled culture. For example, everyone knew that Stumpf did not want to hear bad news or deal with conflict. He attributed that to a preference for "Minnesota Nice." But that, in turn, further motivated those around Stumpf to sweep problems under the rug.[6]

And that's how, as the title of a recent feature article in Vanity Fair put it, "Wells Fargo's cutthroat corporate culture allegedly drove bankers to fraud."[7]

But enough with the negative examples. In this book, we give more airtime to the leaders who get it right. And so we highlight leaders who build productive, robust cultures by broadcasting strong and steady signals on all Five Frequencies.

Here's one: Eric Jones, commissioner of the Detroit Fire Department (DFD).

Jones took over the DFD in 2015 after spending 25 years at the Police Department, where he retired as Assistant Chief of Police. He inherited a Fire Department that was making tentative strides toward recovery in the aftermath of Detroit's bankruptcy. Things had gotten really bad a few years before. In Charlie LeDuff's 2013 non-fictional bestseller, *Detroit: An American Autopsy*, the Fire Department serves as the setting for some of the book's most sobering scenes. Alarms didn't work. Essential equipment was missing. Much of what they did have, such as "melted helmets, boots with holes, coats covered with thick layers of carbon, [made firefighters] the equivalent of walking matchsticks." And yet, all these things had at one point been budgeted. "I began to see it," LeDuff wrote: "$7 million for doorknobs and faucet handles and screen doors that never saw their way to the firehouses. Money just seemed to vanish in the paper shuffle." So, while firefighters brought in their own toilet paper and cleaning supplies, a corrupt mayor (the incarcerated-as-of-this-writing Kwame Kilpatrick) "insinuated that the city firefighters had a bum's job that consisted mainly of sleeping and eating steak, with occasional fire thrown in to pass the time."[8]

Today, in 2019, nobody is yet declaring victory at the Detroit Fire Department. Room for improvement remains, but undeniable progress has been made in the last few years on the important outcome metrics. For example, since 2014, they've cut response times in half, and building fires have decreased by 33 percent. And the Commissioner's culture-shaping efforts—his strong and steady signals across Five Frequencies—have been a driving force behind the progress.

Frequency 1: Leaders' decisions and actions

Jones didn't come up through the ranks of the Fire Department, so he recognized he'd have to work to earn firefighters' trust. They wouldn't be won over with fancy rhetoric. Instead, he said, "You got me. I don't know how to put out a fire. But I am a good steward of budgets. And by being a good steward of the budget, I'm going to get you the training you need. I'm going to get the equipment you need. I'm going to make sure that there are no layoffs. I'm going to do everything that I can to put you in a position to be the best firefighter you can be." And then he proceeded to follow through. They improved training, standardized equipment, purchased new rigs, increased inspections, and more. Jones also broadcast culture-shaping signals by opening all 15 of the appointed positions on his leadership team. The incumbents needed to reapply. He ended up swapping out about half of them, filling those roles with people he was confident were more aligned with his agenda of rigorously driving performance and reshaping culture.

Frequency 2: What leaders reward and recognize

Early on, Jones recognized the department didn't have enough medical first responders. And the ones they did have were often butting heads with their firefighter colleagues. In some cases, the two groups would operate out of the same firehouses, but wouldn't eat together because they didn't consider themselves members of the same team. Jones knows you've got to reward what you want to see more of, so in contract negotiations with the Detroit Firefighters Association they added a 4 percent incentive for anyone who completed a medical first responders' certification. The response was so positive that Detroit now has roughly ten times as many fire companies that are fully staffed to respond to emergencies, whether medical or fire.

Increasing pay is one thing, but what about other forms of recognition? While the stereotype of first responders is that they don't like to show emotion and are indifferent to awards, Jones believes recognition really matters. And he recalled from his days at the Police Department that, "if you did something really great—make a great arrest or prevent a suicide—you might wait seven years before you get a certificate recognizing you for an event you barely remember." To reinforce the behavior he wanted to see more of, he knew he'd need to bring positive consequences closer. So now, on the third Tuesday of the month, he gets from each division head a report of meritorious service. And then once per month they hold an award ceremony for firefighters and their families, an event which is frequently covered by the media.

Another example of Jones' culture-defining signals on Frequency 2: Recently, Commissioner Jones' boss, Detroit Mayor Mike Duggan, asked our team to share some information at one of his cabinet meetings. Commissioner Jones was also on the same agenda to provide an update on significant progress made to strengthen the City's ISO rating (which impacts what residents and businesses pay for fire insurance). Jones could have covered the highlights himself in two slides. But instead, he brought with him, and turned the entire presentation over to, his division heads who'd led the hard work (but typically aren't invited to cabinet meetings). It was riveting, watching them talk—some with more polish than others—about what they'd accomplished and smile modestly (but proudly) as they listened to the Mayor's heartfelt praise.

Frequency 3: What leaders tolerate (or don't)

Jones discovered early on there was little rigor around metrics—and by extension, little accountability. "I sat in meetings where we would speculate about response times or about what equipment we had. But we didn't know. And because we didn't know, we couldn't take a scientific approach to improving our performance," he recalled. So, instituting reliable metrics was an essential first step. That made it possible to isolate, quantify, and solve problems. "For instance," Jones said, "we learned we had way too many missed runs. What's the problem? No accountability around communication technology. That's not acceptable. For starters, we didn't have a way to verify that a run was missed because of broken or malfunctioning equipment. So, we created a communication inspection protocol. Now, every day, firefighters check their printers—but they also check and sign off on six other ways they can be notified of a run. And when a printer, or a mobile phone, or a landline is not working, we get it fixed. Missed runs have almost disappeared." And he has many other examples. It's all about engineering excuses out of the system. "Now we have a culture of measurement," Jones said, "which is making it possible to have a culture of accountability."

Frequency 4: How leaders show up informally

Jones said he learned in the Police Department the importance of engaging the people who are going to implement your plans. "You've got to be willing to listen to their feedback and act on at least some of their input, or your plan is going to fail." So, he recognizes the importance of being an accessible leader. And while Jones was never a Detroit firefighter, his son is. When Jones became Commissioner, he said to his son: "People are going to run things by you and suggest you run them by me. Don't do it. Just give them my number and encourage them to call me directly." Jones also has an open-door policy. "They can come in and talk to me about anything," he said.

Frequency 5: Leaders' formal communications

Jones recognizes the power of a simple narrative about "where we're going and how we'll get there" to rally attention and discretionary energy in support of a righteous cause. One of those causes is his quest for the City to earn an ISO 1 rating. (It's a 10-point scale and the City's current ranking is 4.) The lower the number, the lower the cost of fire insurance, which gives the City leverage to attract new businesses. Jones visited every battalion to present his vision and then discuss what would be required of firefighters to achieve it. He also shared how firefighters and the Fire Department would benefit from seeing the journey through to its destination (as a result of an increased tax base). After every presentation, Jones heard a comment like this: "A lot of times we get stuff from downtown and we're like, 'what the hell is this?' We go through the motions, but we don't understand why we're doing it. But this makes sense. This is exciting." So far, the Fire Department has channeled that excitement and discretionary energy into incredible feats, such as rapid completion of 30,000 fire hydrant inspections and repairs, in pursuit of its ISO 1 vision.

For another example of leaders who get it right, let's go half-way around the world to Singapore, where the Asian Bank DBS is located. DBS originally stood for Development Bank of Singapore. But for many years, people joked that the acronym stood for "Damn Bloody Slow." The lousy customer experiences they delivered earned them the lowest satisfaction scores of any bank in the country.

But today, DBS is widely recognized as Asia's best bank. In ten years, they've gone from worst to first on many customer satisfaction measures. What happened in between? Cultural transformation.

Frequency 1: Leaders' decision and actions

When Piyush Gupta became DBS's CEO in 2009, he committed to make DBS more customer-centric. But how? For one thing, he decided to investigate for himself the bank's long waiting times. "I went to our branches incognito to speak to customers and ascertain for myself the cause of our service issues," he said. "I found out that a significant part of the queue was because we had deliberately created a product to make it inconvenient for customers to withdraw cash at ATMs, in the misguided belief that this would help protect the deposit balances."

Knowing that you tend to manage what you measure, he and his team set targets for eliminating customer waiting time. And then they began to focus process improvements on moving the needle downward. In just one year, DBS eliminated more than 250 million hours in customer waiting time. Customer satisfaction shot up quickly.

Frequency 2: What leaders reward and recognize

DBS thinks of itself as a 26,000-employee startup. Like any other tech startup, that means running lots of experiments—over 1,000 in the past couple of years—to find new ways to deliver value to customers at a profit. The thing about running a thousand experiments is that hundreds of them probably won't work. Recognizing this, good startups know the importance of rewarding and recognizing "failing fast" and learning.

That's not necessarily what banks are known for. But DBS makes learning an explicit part of its employee compact. It goes something like this: If you are not well-equipped with the changing skillsets required in this new digital age, you risk obsolescence. So come here and work hard; be part of some experiments, some of which will work better than others; and try some things that you may struggle with or don't nail right away. The payoff? We're going to help future-proof you and equip you with the experience, exposure, and education to stay ahead of the curve.

For example, when DBS selected Nahariah Mohd Nor, a branch teller in her 40s, to become a service officer on the bank's new video teller machines, she got frustrated with the fast pace and new technology and asked to return to her old job.

The bank's human resource manager said, "It's okay. Wait. Give it six months." She did, and over time her confidence grew.

Six months later, happily settled in her new role, Nahariah said, "I'm glad I took the leap to re-skill myself because I now feel more confident to face the future where technology is changing the way customers bank and transact."

Frequency 3: What leaders tolerate (or don't)

DBS couldn't operate like an agile startup with old, bureaucratic decision-making processes. So, according to Paul Cobban, Chief Data and Transformation Officer, they needed to "shift from individual projects that need approvals and subcommittees, to giving the freedom to a group of people to operate like a platform." As Forbes described it:

> DBS's old decision-making process required people to ask permission from managers via email. Delays in responding or failure to respond altogether were the blockers that impeded progress. To address these blockers, Cobban instituted weekly decision-making meetings that brought all interested parties together. "Teams present their ideas to decision-makers in person," Cobban says. "99% of the time they get a yes answer on the spot."

Frequency 4: How leaders show up informally

"Informal" is a good way to describe how leaders show up with their employees at DBS. According to CEO Gupta, "We've done away with cubicles, so in large parts of the bank it's all open space. People stand up, conduct 'agile' meetings, place post-its on the walls, and huddle together in scrums every morning."

Leaders lead most effectively in agile environments when they operate from a creative mindset that helps them coach their people toward important outcomes, rather than a reactive mindset where egos and hierarchy too often get in the way. Recognizing this, Cobban says, "we took our leaders and put them in 'hackathons' with startups. Hackathons replaced the executive training budget."

What's a hackathon? Says Gupta, "This involved taking seven or eight DBS employees and forming them into a joint team with a couple of people from a start-up company. We had about 20 teams of this size and put them through a five-day hackathon process, with one day devoted to understanding technology and skill building in human-centered design, then three days or so of working together with start-up kits to help the teams code and create an app. We gave them mattresses, Ping-Pong tables, and free-flowing beer, but at the end of 72 hours they had to have an app. On the final day, they would showcase these apps to a judging team. In many cases, people came up with fairly good creative solutions, but the real power came from the experience of recognizing that you could do things differently and have a real impact."

By the way, Gupta role models from the top the open, easy way of showing up with employees that he wants all DBS leaders to emulate. "Tell Piyush" is an online forum where employees can freely share their feedback and post their questions. Piyush personally responds to all the questions and comments raised (directing them to others for follow up where appropriate).

Frequency 5: Leaders' formal communications

Gupta says that it's important to give people a sense of direction, describing where we're going and how we'll get there. In terms of "where we're going," the DBS rally cry is "Become the D in GANDALF." What does that mean?

According to CIO David Gledhill, "The first letters of Google, Amazon, Netflix, Apple, LinkedIn, and Facebook together spell GANALF. That was missing a D, and we, as DBS, fortunately have a D. So, our mission became how to become the D in GANDALF."

"Now that might sound a little cheesy," he said, "but in actual fact, it was an amazing rallying call to our people. It had a bigger impact on our technology people and many other people in the organization than anything else we've done, because it started to make them think about what was possible. It got them to think, 'we're not acting like another bank, and here's how we really start to transform ourselves like a technology company.'"

As for "how we get there," the rally cry is for DBS to always show up as RED: Respectful, Easy to deal with, Dependable.

When you "have a message on a single page that everybody can easily grasp," Gledhill says, "then you have something very powerful that you can start to push on. And with RED, it was very clear, something people could act on, and that drove massive change through the organization."

With strong and steady signals across the Five Frequencies, DBS has come a long way from its "Damn Bloody Slow" days. But its leaders continue to treat their stewardship of culture as mission critical.

Says Gupta, "Today, we are up against businesses that work out of a garage, take risks, operate in a nimble way, and have a different kind of energy and drive. Large incumbent companies that can't create a similar kind of culture just won't be able to compete."

For our third example, let's take a U-turn from Asia-Pacific back to Detroit, where Cindy Pasky founded Strategic Staffing Solutions (S3) in 1990 with five employees. Today, S3 is a $300+ million company with 3,600 consultants providing IT and business services in 49 out of 50 U.S. states and 15 countries.

How have Cindy and her team driven that growth? Relentless customer-centricity driven by a culture of strong tribal affiliation. The S3 tribe is demanding. If you work there, you're expected to work hard, but it also means you get be part of something special, an organization that invests in its people and makes a real difference in its communities.

From the start, Cindy has cultivated S3 culture as a source of competitive advantage. Here are some examples of how S3 has created and spread S3 culture with strong and steady signals across the Five Frequencies.

Frequency 1: Leaders' decisions and actions

Cindy hires for character and trains for skill. But what kind of character? To deliver the customer experience S3 wants to be known for, employees have to know how to respond quickly, work in teams, and be willing to put it all on the line. Recognizing that military service promotes these character traits, Cindy implemented a veterans hiring program. Today, veterans and their families comprise 56 percent of the S3 workforce. It's a way of honoring service and strengthening communities—and it's good business.

A few years ago, Cindy dyed her hair green—the corporate color—for the annual meeting. It has stayed green ever since. Unless the tribal affiliation in your company rivals S3's, you're unlikely to follow her lead. But at S3, Cindy's green hair symbolizes a consistent and shared commitment to delivering the brand to customers.

One of Cindy's ultimate measures of success is "people working well in roles they've never filled before." To that end, Cindy's distinctive coif has helped S3 recruit for character: Some of S3's best employees include a waiter from a restaurant located in the headquarters building, a parking attendant from the garage downstairs, and a doorman at the Detroit Athletic Club—all of whom took the initiative to "ask the lady with the green hair" if she was hiring. She said, "send me your resume." When they did, she evaluated them and made the hires. These decisions: (1) advanced S3's commitment to offering people an opportunity to succeed and change their station in life and (2) were good for business, too.

Frequency 2: What leaders reward and recognize

S3 rewards hard work and results. High performers and their spouses take some great S3 vacations, for example.

But it's more than that. Because of the strong tribal affiliation, there's an explicit emphasis on promoting from within. And if you work hard and well enough to belong to the S3 tribe, the tribe will have your back when something bad happens.

For example, in the aftermath of Hurricane Katrina, a team member went to New Orleans from Detroit to deliver cash to employees (ATMs didn't work) and ensure their safety. When an employee in Philadelphia lost everything in a housefire, Cindy's executive assistant showed up right away to ensure this employee and his family had a place to stay and got back on their feet…all before buying them a house.

Another part of the emotional rewards of working for S3 is knowing you're part of a company that makes a real difference in the community. S3 gives over $2 million annually for causes, and not just the ones Cindy cares about, such as the Michigan Humane Society. S3 is also generous to causes championed by its employees.

As one employee told us, "Some people call S3 a cult. We even gave out green Kool-Aid one year, so we get the joke. But, it's a good cult. We don't do anything bad: we support workforce development, education, giving back to the community, and veterans and their families. What's wrong with a cult like that?"

Frequency 3: What leaders tolerate (or don't)

A tribe can't maintain its strength and resilience if it's sloppy about what it tolerates. If you're an S3 employee not playing to win as a team or jumping through hoops to deliver customer value, you can expect a coaching conversation about that. If you fail to learn from mistakes or don't work hard, you probably won't last. It wouldn't be fair to the rest of the tribe. And while S3 gives a lot to charity, *it* is not a charity. S3 has a lot of business performance metrics, and expects employees to hit their targets. If you miss them, you'll be supported and coached to close the gap, but if that doesn't work, the tribe's not for you.

Frequency 4: How leaders show up informally

No one has a door on their office, including Cindy. She's continually roaming the halls and visiting the company's various sites. "You can expect to find Cindy in your office at any time," an employee told us. She responds to emails within four hours.

The open and transparent information flow has helped create a climate where people feel empowered to speak up, innovate, and take action. "Cindy makes it safe for people to experiment with ways to deliver more customer value," an employee named Mary said. "She doesn't want people to ask for permission. She creates an environment where people know what matters and then she lets people do it." Creating a culture where employees know they have a lot of freedom means employees also give more discretionary effort than if S3 leaders specified every detail. The employee continued, "But because I get autonomy, it means I don't want to disappoint Cindy or the rest of the team."

Frequency 5: Leader's formal communications

S3's formal communication is marked by ritualistic consistency. Since the outset, S3 has operated from the idea that its success is supported by four pillars:

- Set the bar high for what a company should do

- Create jobs

- Provide people with the opportunity to succeed and change their station in life

- Make charitable giving and community work a core part of our business

When employees tune into Cindy's regular live-streams of "State of S3" meetings or other channels, they see leaders explicitly connecting the dots between these four pillars and the company's performance, decisions, and actions. The consistency helps draw people into the tribal narrative and keep them there.

The S3 formula isn't for everyone. But for Cindy Pasky and her team, managing culture as a source of competitive advantage has produced an average annual growth rate of 19 percent.

Commissioner Jones, the top team at DBS, and Cindy Pasky are leaders we admire. And there are many others. We'll highlight in the coming pages dozens of examples of leaders who've shaped culture as a source of competitive advantage—and minimized the risk that "culture eats strategy for breakfast."

- Chapter 1 describes how leaders shape culture through their decisions and actions (**Frequency 1**). As you'll see, it's about showing more than telling, role modeling what you want to see more of, and being "long-term greedy."

- You always get more of what you reward and recognize. So, if there's something about current performance you don't like, you've got to take a hard look at the signals you're broadcasting on **Frequency 2**. In chapter 2, we share what behavioral economists say about making your rewards and recognition truly motivating.

- Leaders and cultures are ultimately defined by what they tolerate (**Frequency 3**). Chapter 3 describes how leaders send strong and steady signals on this frequency, even when it's unpleasant.

- Chapter 4 describes how leaders shape culture by how they show up informally (**Frequency 4**). This is about building trust and affiliation, which in turn makes it easier to confront and solve problems—without egos and BS getting in the way.

- Sometimes leaders think they can shape a strong culture simply with a robust formal communication program (**Frequency 5**). We know this doesn't work. But that doesn't mean the fifth frequency is unimportant, either. In Chapter 5, we describe how the most effective leaders broadcast strong and steady signals through their formal communications. In the process, they effectively "compete for attention," in part by pulling employees into a compelling storyline. This amplifies the signals they're deliberately broadcasting on the other four frequencies.

And then in Chapter 6, we highlight the other half of our framework for helping leaders turn culture into competitive advantage.

You can't manage what you don't measure. That's why leaders who are genuinely committed to shifting culture for competitive advantage establish a culture metric that's a reliable leading indicator of actual business performance. And then they work on moving the needle, with strong and steady signals on Five Frequencies. Follow-up assessments show what's working and why—so leaders can double-down on what's effective, and recalibrate what isn't. It's agile, "fit for purpose," experimental, and outcome-focused. So working on culture is never just a "check-the-box" HR initiative. Instead, the most effective leaders treat culture-shifting as a serious business process that's explicitly tied to business results.

CHAPTER 1
FREQUENCY 1: YOUR DECISIONS AND ACTIONS

FIVE FREQUENCIES

Frequency 1: Your decisions and actions

This chapter covers four signal boosts for turning culture into competitive advantage

- **Show more than tell**
- **Role model what you want to see more of**
- **Remember, if it costs you nothing, it's not a "value"**
- **Go long-term greedy**

According to political journalists Jim Vandehei and Mike Allen, "All habits, good and bad—in all organizations, big and small—flow down fast from the top."[1] They happened to be talking about how President

Trump's lifelong habits have quickly shaped the culture of the White House, federal agencies, and the party he leads.

But the principle is universal. You are constantly transmitting culture-defining messages through your decisions and actions—intentionally or not. That's why it's important to self-monitor your signals and be deliberate in what you broadcast—so that you produce culture "by design" rather than "by default."

This chapter covers four Signal Boosts that will help you do that.

Signal Boost #1: Show more than tell

CEO Trent Kimball looks into the camera and announces he stands behind his product. But then he sits instead. In a marketing video watched millions of times on YouTube, Trent crouches on a stool behind a bulletproof windshield manufactured by his company, Texas Armoring Corporation. One of Trent's employees stands a short distance away and points a loaded AK-47 at his boss. The employee might be nervous, but Trent appears calm and confident. The employee aims his rifle at Trent and fires three times. The windshield absorbs all three bullets. Unscathed, Trent emerges from behind the shattered-but-fully-intact windshield and again looks into the camera to deliver a short marketing pitch. The words aren't memorable. But they don't have to be. Trent's action has already told you everything you need to know: Texas Armoring sells one hell of a product.

Trent's bold actions, however, aren't limited to marketing videos. In fact, bold behavior has been a defining feature of his leadership from day one. A deposit from Texas Armoring's first customer financed the start up, but that worked only because Trent waited six months to take a paycheck. More recently, he committed the organization to a strategy of global growth, and then he backed up his words by moving his entire family of eleven to Honduras. Actions like these have helped Texas Armoring attract new talent, retain A Players, and motivate discretionary energy.

But you know what's less interesting than how Trent leads? Apparently, how Trent *talks* about it. As of this writing, a two-year-old YouTube video of Trent talking to BYU business school students has 117 views. Turns out Trent is better at "showing" than "telling."

And that puts him in *very* good company. According to our research, it's a leadership trait shared by most leaders who turn culture into competitive advantage.

By the way, this coaching point— "show more than tell"—isn't just an invitation to behave boldly. It's also about more mundane things like zealously following through on commitments and doing what you say you're going to do. It's about sustaining the focus on stated priorities even when it's boring and other shiny objects and executive brain candy are competing for your attention. In short, it's about remembering what we learned in first grade: Actions speak louder than words.

Signal Boost #2: Role model what you want to see more of

Dr. Reginald Eadie was lying on his back on a patient bed in the Hematology Department of Harper University Hospital, one of two urban hospitals he presided over as CEO.[*] He wasn't sick. He was role modeling. And he wasn't role modeling naptime, either.

He'd invited us to join him on his regular morning rounds, visiting not with patients but with teams of employees, engaging them around their current performance metrics and their efforts to continuously improve them.

The team was performing well, hitting their targets, checking the boxes on all the things the Joint Commission (the organization that accredits hospitals) would look at when they came out to evaluate the hospital. He'd offered the team heartfelt kudos before hopping on the bed and gazing at the ceiling.

"Looking at things from the Joint Commission's perspective is not exactly the same thing as looking at what we do from the patient's perspective," Dr. Eadie said. And looking at the hospital experience from the patient's perspective—and literally so—is what he wanted to role model.

Standing around Dr. Eadie, the Hematology team joined him in looking at the ceiling. "What do you see?" he asked. The answer came quickly: "There's a ceiling tile that needs to be fixed." The team readily

---

[*] Dr. Eadie is now the CEO of Trinity Health of New England.

agreed that "staring at a broken ceiling tile is not something we want for our patients" and they captured next actions for getting it fixed.

Later, we asked Dr. Eadie to elaborate on what we'd observed. "When the Joint Commission comes in to inspect a hospital, they care about cleanliness. So, we'll do a high dusting test. (High dusting is the process of keeping clean all difficult to reach areas. To clinicians, it means removing disease causing agents like bacteria.) And it's necessary. But it's not enough. Because you know who doesn't do high dusting? The patient. The patient isn't thinking about high dusting. What they do care about is what they're looking at when they're lying on a hospital bed."

That's why, when he's conducting his rounds to engage front-line teams on performance, he'll hop up on beds and share what he sees. It's also why you might see him being pushed on a gurney around the hospital. "You'd be surprised," he says, "how much a small bump in the hallway turns into an uncomfortable speed bump when you're on your back. We also know that you experience sound differently on a gurney. I've also been pushed and have pushed others in a wheelchair—so we can experience what you see, hear, and experience at the nurse's station or anywhere else. You don't fully know what's unpleasant and how to fix it until you experience the hospital from the patient's perspective."

But the point isn't for Dr. Eadie to do all these patient-experience-based inspections himself. The point is to role model the behavior he wants to see more of. And it works. "Throughout the hospital, we see employees looking more closely at the patients' experiences through *their* eyes and ears. And when that happens, patient satisfaction improves."

That's not the only time we saw Dr. Eadie role modeling the behavior he wanted to see more of. On another occasion, he decided he wanted his leadership team to give more candid feedback to one another about performance.

"I saw we weren't being fully honest with one another," he said. Why? "I suspected our team didn't have enough experience giving constructive feedback that didn't cause a defensive response. So, the excuse was: 'Why be honest if it only results in unpleasantness?'"

Dr. Eadie knew it was up to him to role model doing it right, which is why when the hospital got ready for the next round of performance evaluations, he said, "I'm going first."

Under his direction, all hospital leaders gathered input from their respective departments about Dr. Eadie's performance as hospital president. Informed by that feedback, the team anonymously evaluated their leader and gave him a score.

"And then we got together to review the evaluation and talk about it," Dr. Eadie said. "I asked questions to better understand the opportunities for improvement without getting defensive. I tried to demonstrate curiosity. And when someone raised their hand to explain why they gave me a low score in one area, I thanked them for it."

But it didn't end there. He built an action plan that included the launch of a monthly colleague and physician recognition program; more frontline input on decision making; and increased leadership visibility.

Over three years, this approach—and the behaviors required to make it successful—cascaded throughout the organization. "We got more honest about our performance," Dr. Eadie said. "This led to lower but more realistic performance evaluations. Now those who get low scores are coached up or coached out." This moved the needle on culture, as evidenced by safety culture, engagement, and physician satisfaction scores. "In turn," Eadie says, "that helped us provide better care and service to our patients and their families," as evidenced by increased patient experience scores and organic growth.

$$\S\S\S\S$$

As Captain D. Michael Abrashoff wrote in *It's Your Ship: Management Techniques from the Best Damn Ship in the Navy*, "You train your crew how to operate through every decision you make and every action you take. If they see you not telling the truth, they may feel free to lie as well. Likewise, if they see you challenge outdated business practices, they will follow suit. Doing so will become ingrained in the culture."[2]

You probably agree. But are you confident you're already flawlessly role modeling the behavior you want to see more of? Here's a data point that makes the case for sober self-reflection: According to a recent McKinsey study of business transformations, 86 percent of senior executives believe that they are actively demonstrating the change they want employees to make. But only 53 percent of employees see it that way.[3]

Signal Boost #3: Remember, if it costs you nothing, it's not a "value"

Most organizations have a list of stated values that they display prominently. Often, these pronouncements of "Our Values" emerge from an executive retreat where a facilitator led the senior team through the ritual of identifying the concepts with which they'd like to imagine themselves associated ("integrity," "fun," "teamwork," etc.).

It can be powerful when senior leaders (and their consultants) frame this conversation within the context of "this is how we're committing to operate *even* when it's really inconvenient and costs us something." But too often, they don't, which results in an exercise that is largely self-indulgent and narcissistic.

Here's an example. Some years ago, when Andy Serwer wrote the "Street Life" column for *Fortune*, a reader wrote him:

> Just a quick note from down in the trenches. I work for an e-consultancy and a while back the Culture Committee came up with a list of the company's core values. To keep them fresh in our mind a hat that exemplified each value was purchased and given to a person that had demonstrated that core value and has been passed on to a new recipient at the company's quarterly meeting. Well, things have gotten a little lean on the demand side in the industry and this week right before the quarterly meeting there was a layoff. The bad news: Integrity, Teamwork, Fun, and Respect for the Individual will soon be working for someone else.

But two hat-wearers—Growth and Innovation—kept their jobs, revealing what senior leaders *really* valued all along.

As author Nassim Taleb says, "There is a difference between beliefs that are decorative and different sorts of beliefs, those that map to action…How much you truly 'believe' in something can be manifested only through what you are willing to risk for it."[4] We've seen this time and again. In fact, so many leadership teams (and their consultants) have failed to properly frame their "values" discussions that this term has become bastardized, largely divorced from its economic origins, where "value" is defined as "what you're willing to pay for."

An example: A client of ours led a division of a well-known technology company that said they valued "playing to win as a team." But it didn't come naturally for people. So, this executive, whenever he identified a big problem, assigned people from at least two different functions to work together on it. In most cases, this wasn't the most efficient way to solve the problem, so it literally cost him something to go about it this way. But he wanted to invest in cooperation and communication across boundaries, until living the value "of playing to win as a team" occurred more organically in his organization's culture.

Of course, paying for something sometimes means "putting your money where your mouth is." But just as often, you show you truly value something when it costs you other very finite resources like your attention and energy.

Our friend Jeff Rocke recalls that one of his mentors, a division president at Kaiser Permanente, once received a complaint from a group advocating for the rights of the those with disabilities. A Kaiser Permanente patient had contacted them criticizing the lack of disability-friendly architecture and medical equipment in the facility.

The president was about to pass the complaint off to Legal with a note asking them to send an obligatory response. But then, instead, he reached out by phone to personally speak with the complainants. The result was ongoing discussions and a partnership. Their representatives came in to that facility to retrofit it for people with disabilities, and they developed a strategy to ensure that all facilities were brought up to standards based on consultation with the advocacy group. He demonstrated that the organization valued "caring," regardless of whether that was stated on any posters.

Employees know that one of your most scarce resources is your time. So, what you're willing to spend it on sends powerful culture-shifting signals. Case in point: When Brad Sawatzke became Chief Nuclear Officer of Energy Northwest, he was very impressed with the fact that the people he met *did* want to change. They were tired of poor performance and were willing to do what it took.

He knew that was a good place to start, but said Brad, "I next needed everyone to operate from a consistent set of expectations and standard behaviors. So, we rolled out an Excellence Model describing expected behaviors and developed a phased approach to improvement, recognizing that everything cannot be completed at once. We decided to use a half-day training to push the Excellence Model out to our 1,000-plus employees. To help ensure we made it stick, I taught the class myself."

Brad understood that his people needed to feel that he believed in what he was talking about. Sure—any good trainer could have covered the material, but he needed everyone to understand *his conviction*. And so he taught. Additionally, in the years since, he's done refresher training twice. Only on the third round of training did he hand some of it off to other senior leaders.

Has it worked? According to Brad, now elevated to CEO, the plant's running better, and over the last five years they've set a record every year for megawatt production.

We've covered money, attention, and time. Sometimes what living your values means is you take on the risk of ruffling feathers. CEO Nick Akins shared a couple of examples of what that has looked like at American Electric Power, the midwestern utility he leads.

- When he became president of one of the operating companies (before becoming CEO), he learned that an expectation of the role was to participate in one of the important clubs in town. He also learned that the club had no minorities in it. Nick said, "Fix that and I'll join. They did…and I did."

- When AEP rolled out employee resource groups—and particularly when they rolled out the LGBT employee resource group—they talked about it openly. The feedback on the company blog was extremely negative. So, Nick sent a letter out to everyone defining his expectations of AEP's culture. "I said if you cannot accommodate an open, collaborative, diverse workforce then you need to find something else to do."

Signal Boost #4: Go "long-term greedy."

In the 1970's, one of the big names on Wall Street stood apart: Goldman Sachs. Gus Levy, the firm's managing partner, was asked what made the culture so special. "At Goldman Sachs," Levy responded, "we're greedy, but we're *long-term* greedy." What he meant was that the firm sought always to advance its own self-interests; their enviable culture wasn't a function of altruistic do-goodism. But the time horizon for calculating ROI wasn't days, weeks, or even quarters—it was years, and maybe decades.

And he meant it. Stories that demonstrated the "long-term greedy" ethos became part of the firm's folklore. For example, after the stock market crashed in 1987, Goldman Sachs faced a $100 million loss at the time, 20 percent of the firm's earnings—on an underwriting deal to partially privatize British Petroleum. When some of the underwriters began looking for legal technicalities that would reduce their exposure, Goldman Sachs' managing partner at the time, John Weinburg, pushed back:

> Gentlemen, Goldman Sachs is going to do this [deal]. It is expensive and painful, but we are going to do it. Because...those of you who decide not to do it...won't be underwriting a goat house. Not even an outhouse.

And when the resulting loss chased other large firms out of the privatization business in Europe, Goldman Sachs picked up the slack. Long-term greedy paid off. During that same era, Goldman Sachs left short-term money on the table when it refused to represent any company undertaking a hostile bid for another company. Threatened companies, in turn, took their business to Goldman Sachs. Another win for long-term greedy. As the firm grew and grew, this folklore helped untold numbers of employees navigate sticky situations: "We should do the right thing even if it hurts in the short-term, because at Goldman Sachs we're long-term greedy."[5]

But in 1999 Goldman Sachs went public. Predictably, the investors who bought shares of the company were more myopic than the partners had been. Over the next decade, the focus on delivering quarterly performance to the market eroded the culture of "long-term greedy."

In the years leading up to the Great Recession and Wall Street Bailout, all the Wall Street firms, including Goldman Sachs, paid their traders based on "...profits or fee generation, regardless of the outcome down the road," according to writer Nick Paumgarten. "You had an incentive to generate inflated or ephemeral gains and, often, little incentive not to." He adds: "The amazing thing about the piggishness [that led the financial crisis] is that, in a certain light, most people, according to the strictures of their self-interest (whether enlightened or not), behaved rationally."[6] Yep, they were greedy. *Short-term* greedy.

Goldman Sachs' CEO Lloyd Blankfein later owned up to it. After paying back the firm's $10 billion government bailout, he conceded that "we participated in the market euphoria and failed to raise a responsible voice" in the lead-up to the financial crisis. He added:

"Real stability can return only if our industry accepts that certain practices were unhealthy and not in the long-term interests of individual institutions and the financial system as a whole."[7] His predecessor, Gus Levy, probably could have used fewer words to say the same thing: "It's time to return to 'long-term greed.'"

LTG Today. More recently, Larry Fink, CEO at BlackRock, the world's largest investor, has become an advocate of looking long-term, in spheres both financial and political. In a letter to the CEOs of the S&P 500,[8] Fink wrote:

> I have written to the CEOs of leading companies urging resistance to the powerful forces of short-termism afflicting corporate behavior.
>
> We are asking that every CEO lay out for shareholders each year a strategic framework for long-term value creation…Without clearly articulated plans, companies risk losing the faith of long-term investors. …Over time, as companies do a better job laying out their long-term growth frameworks, the need diminishes for quarterly EPS guidance, and we would urge companies to move away from providing it. Today's culture of quarterly earnings hysteria is totally contrary to the long-term approach we need.

Then the critique pivots to politicians:

> Public officials must adopt policies that will support long-term value creation. Companies, for their part, must recognize that while advocating for more infrastructure or comprehensive tax reform may not bear fruit in the next quarter or two, the absence of effective long-term policies in these areas undermines the economic ecosystem in which companies function—and with it, their chances for long-term growth.

When BlackRock's Larry Fink said CEOs should scrap quarterly EPS guidance and take a long-term strategic view, he could have pointed out that one prominent CEO had already done just that. Unilever CEO Paul Polman made this choice his first day on the job back in 2009. "If we do the right things then we do them for the longer term," he'd said. "We have to get out of this quarterly rat race, this expectation management versus reality. And that's a business model that's not run by quarters; that's a business model that's run by years."[9] Further, he's invited investors who don't "buy into this long-term value creation model…which is sustainable," to go elsewhere. He's also said he doesn't want to be labeled "courageous" because he's simply advancing the rational but long-term self-interests of shareholders, employees, and customers.[10]

Amazon's Jeff Bezos is another CEO who has demonstrated a willingness to "plant seeds that take seven years to bear fruit." As he's explained, "If we needed to see meaningful financial results in two to three years, some of the most meaningful things we've done we would never have even started. Things like Kindle, things like Amazon Web Services, Amazon Prime. The list of such things is long at Amazon."[11]

The forefather of long-term greedy—and a darn good chocolatier.

Decades before Gus Levy coined the phrase "long-term greedy," Milton Hershey was practicing it. While his contemporaries (such "Robber Barons" as Carnegie, Rockefeller, and Vanderbilt) extracted the most amount of work from employees for the least amount of money, Hershey took a more enlightened view. He invested heavily in the infrastructure of what became Hershey, Pennsylvania so that his employees would love where they lived. And when the Great Depression came, he invested even more—in schools, libraries, theaters, roads, and more—which meant jobs.

"Legend has it that during construction of the hotel, Hershey was watching a steam shovel in operation when a foreman proudly commented that it could do the job of 40 workers. Hershey told the foreman to get rid of the shovel and hire 40 workers."[12] All the while, Hershey maintained profitability. And after the Depression ended, powered by a loyal workforce, Hershey flourished.

Every leader can go "long-term greedy." Sure, regardless of the persuasiveness of Fink's argument, this book won't have many readers who can single-handedly change the culture of Wall Street or Washington, D.C. But any leader can shape culture positively by going long-term greedy in her or his own span of control.

For instance, what do you do when you encounter a Moment of Truth—a situation where you know what you're supposed to do—but due to productivity or other pressures you're tempted to do something else? As Gus Levy suggested earlier in the chapter, he avoided taking shortcuts not just because "it's the right thing to do" but because it's good business, viewed from a long-term perspective. The payoff associated with "doing the right thing" takes the form of reputational and brand equity, valuable relationships, smoother, more predictable operations, and competitive advantage in the recruitment and retention of top talent. (Of course, for this payoff to occur, long-term greedy leaders must also hold their people accountable to high standards; more on this in Chapter 3.)

But going long-term greedy isn't just about your ethics. For example, it has implications for how you select and develop people. Do you actively hire people smarter than you? There's a short-term cost to your ego: You give up the opportunity to be the smartest person in the room. The long-term payoff is a stronger, higher-performing team. Do you delegate as much important work as possible? It's costly in the short run. You give up time you don't have to equip others to do something they won't do exactly the way you'd do it yourself. Painful. But the long-term payoff is that your people know how to perform…so you can focus on your highest and best use. And what about when those performers have opportunities to move onto bigger and better assignments elsewhere. The short-term greedy leader stands in the way. She or he doesn't want to have to recruit and develop a new person to fill the role. Long-term greedy leaders recognize that supporting the people they've helped develop to move on fosters a reputation that attracts new A Players.

What else do long-term greedy leaders do? They're not impulsive. They believe that "speed wins" but it also kills. They assess risks. They invest time to listen to stakeholders, reflect on what they've heard, and make informed decisions. The payoff is less rework and higher-quality decision-making.

Long-term greedy leaders are also committed to learning from mistakes. They lead their teams in "after action reviews" to capture "lessons learned" at the completion of every major milestone or initiative. These take time and are sometimes unpleasant: After all, who among us relishes a collective meditation on what went wrong? But the payoff is a learning, continuously improving team that actively converts its mistakes into hard-won intellectual capital.

An emerging case study: LTG at Uber. We were just talking about acknowledging mistakes and apologizing for them. It's nobody's formula for fun—but it's often part of the formula for long-term greedy. And it's what Uber's new CEO Dara Khosrowshahi did to signal the beginning of a cultural transformation shortly after his arrival in 2017. Under the leadership of their original CEO, Travis Kalanick, Uber developed a "bro-culture" that tolerated and, in some cases, celebrated sexual harassment and legal non-compliance. According to the company's own data, many drivers considered the company "as made up of a bunch of greedy, self-centered jerks." The defining feature of Kalanick's leadership was "unrelenting combativeness." In response to any raised eyebrows, Kalanick protested that Uber had a PR problem, not a cultural one.[13]

According to an astonishing Bloomberg exposé,[14] Uber executives were arguing with Kalanick over this very issue when they learned of a damaging video posted online. The video showed Kalanick combatively arguing with an Uber driver, Fawzi Kamel, over rates.[15] When it went viral, Kalanick was persuaded to meet with Kamel for a five-minute meeting to apologize. Apparently, Kalanick couldn't pull that off. Instead, he spent more than an hour resuming the debate with Kamel, ultimately offering him compensation as a means of putting the issue behind them.

When the board finally brought in Khosrowshahi to replace Kalanick, there was plenty of challenges for the new CEO to tackle. Just weeks into Khosrowshahi's tenure, the City of London banned the service. Instead of resorting to Kalanick-style combativeness,

Khosrowshahi offered sober reflection. In an open letter,[16] he wrote: "While Uber has revolutionized the way people move in cities around the world, it's equally true that we've gotten things wrong along the way. On behalf of everyone at Uber globally, I apologize for the mistakes we've made." He added: "…we will look to be long-term partners with the cities we serve; and we will run our business with humility, integrity and passion."

He also wrote to employees:[17]

> While the impulse may be to say that [the London ban] is unfair, one of the lessons I've learned over time is that change comes from self-reflection. So, it's worth examining how we got here. The truth is that there is a high cost to a bad reputation. Irrespective of whether we did everything that is being said about us in London today (and to be clear, I don't think we did), it really matters what people think of us, especially in a global business like ours, where actions in one part of the world can have serious consequences in another. Going forward, it's critical that we…[build] trust through our actions and our behavior.

A few months later, he had more to say in a LinkedIn post:[18]

> [It's] clear that the culture and approach that got Uber where it is today is not what will get us to the next level. As we move from an era of growth at all costs to one of responsible growth, our culture needs to evolve.

This is what long-term greedy is all about. But—returning to this chapter's first coaching point—we'll now watch to see whether he continues to show more than tell. Will he actually reward the behavior he wants to see more of? What will he stop tolerating?

Frequencies 2 and 3—which refer to what leaders reward and what they tolerate—go a long way toward defining culture and determining whether it's an asset or liability. These frequencies are the focus of the next two chapters.

Signal Boost Summary

Want to turn your culture into a source of competitive advantage? Focus on four Frequency 1 Signal Boosts:

- **Show more than tell:** This isn't just about behaving boldly. It's also about more mundane things like zealously following through on commitments and doing what you say you're going to do. It's about sustaining the focus on stated priorities even when it's boring and other shiny objects and executive brain candy are competing for your attention. In short, it's about remembering what we learned in first grade: Actions speak louder than words.

- **Role model what you want to see more of:** Be clear about your expectations—then exemplify them.

- **Remember, if it costs you nothing, it's not a "value":** Too many have forgotten this word's origins in micro-economics, which is the study of trade-offs. Parting with scarce resources (like money, time, convenience, and attention) demonstrates precisely what you value most.

- **Go long-term greedy:** Calculate the ROI on your decisions and actions based on a time horizon that extends beyond the end-of-quarter. This can mean avoiding ethical shortcuts, hiring people smarter than you, delegating more, and helping prepare high performers for success beyond your team.

CHAPTER 2
FREQUENCY 2: WHAT YOU REWARD AND RECOGNIZE

FIVE FREQUENCIES

Frequency 2: What you reward and recognize

This chapter covers two signal boosts for turning culture into competitive advantage

- **Reward what you want to see more of**
- **Understand the emotional algorithms that motivate your people**

"Whether dealing with monkeys, rats, or human beings," management professor Steven Kerr wrote in 1975, "it is hardly controversial to state that most organisms seek information concerning what activities are rewarded and then seek to do (or at least pretend to do) these things, often to the virtual exclusion of activities not rewarded." The implication? If you want your people to do some particular thing, you'd better reinforce it with "warm signals." It's folly, Kerr said, to "reward A while hoping for B."[1]

Three decades later, he wrote a book[2] about the problem's persistence: Organizations want long-term performance, he noted, but they reward employees who achieve quarterly targets. What they get, predictably, is short-term thinking and number gaming. Or they want teamwork and cooperation but reward only individual goal attainment, leading, predictably, to unproductive competition.

Meanwhile, Harvard Business School's Amy Edmondson has found that organizations say they want a culture of continuous learning, but they don't get it when they rate as top performers "those who silently do what they're told and what has always been done—and don't annoy their superiors with complaints and questions about flawed practices."[3] Other researchers found that while leaders almost universally claim to prize efficiency…

> Employees who start big programs are often celebrated, but rarely those who end old, obsolete and ineffective programs and practices. And managers who lord over big teams and keep adding underlings are rewarded with prestigious titles and big raises—even when their ever-expanding army of bureaucrats adds unnecessary rules and procedures that sap time and energy from people who do the most important work.[4]

The phenomenon of misaligned incentives isn't limited to organizational reward systems, of course. In Jeff's first book, *Leadership without Excuses*, a health care CEO wrote a sidebar lamenting the sickness of the American system:

We all like to think of our caregivers as good people—trying very hard to do the right thing. That is, I believe, actually very true. Our care providers are good people, all trying to do the right thing—but a bit more specifically, everyone is doing the "billable right thing." If it isn't billable, it isn't happening, successfully.

And author Nassim Taleb, in his recent manifesto titled *Skin in the Game*,[5] was surely talking about consultants (among others) when he wrote:

> People who are…compensated to find complicated solutions do not have an incentive to implement simplified ones. In other words, many problems in society come from the interventions of people who sell complicated solutions because that's what their position and training invite them to do. There is absolutely no gain for someone in such a position to propose something simple: you are rewarded for perception, not results. Meanwhile, they pay no price for the side effects…

Now, back to leaders and culture…and more of Kerr's pull-no-punches advice: You know you've got a good reward system, he wrote, if "it gets you what you want." If that's not the case, don't blame your employees; blame your reward system. "The bad news" for leaders, he said, "is that you are responsible for the dysfunctional behaviors that so bother you."[6]

This advice is apparently very hard to implement. After all, Kerr was a senior advisor at Goldman Sachs in the period leading up to the financial crisis. In the aftermath, as you read in the last chapter, Goldman Sachs' CEO went to Congress, after taking a $10 billion bailout, and confessed to mis-aligned reward systems. In other words, even with Kerr on the payroll, the firm "rewarded A while hoping for B."

That's sobering. But the good news? There are plenty of other leaders who *have* pulled off the tough task of rewarding what they want to see more of.

Signal Boost #1: Reward the behavior you want to see more of

Our favorite story on this topic is about Alan Mulally's transformation of Ford's culture—and business performance.[7] When he came on as CEO, he brought with him the alignment process that had worked so well for him at Boeing. It involved his team putting together comprehensive color-coded scorecards on their business performance and then reviewing them together every Thursday. Introducing this approach, Mulally invoked the values of honesty and transparency. The way to solve problems, he said, is to first make them visible.

He got lots of nodding heads. Honesty and transparency were values talked about frequently at Ford. The problem: Those values weren't what Ford had actually been rewarding.

So when Mulally brought his team together to review their performance, their scorecards showed nothing but green.

He was patient for a few weeks because they were learning a new system. But then he called them out: How can we be losing $17 billion this year and still have nothing but greens on our scorecards?

Still, no one relented. Finally, one executive, Mark Fields, decided to give it a try. He was responsible for the rollout of the new Ford Edge, just a few weeks out, and test drivers were reporting a suspension problem. So Fields walked into the next weekly review meeting with a red on his scorecard.

His presentation was met with an audible gasp, as Field's colleagues anticipated the public execution they were about to witness. Instead, they heard applause. From Mullaly. *He was rewarding the behavior he wanted to see more of.*

After Fields explained the problem, Mulally asked: "Who can help?" A couple of hands went up, with colleagues offering suggestions and support. Great! Problem-solving, after all, was the point of the exercise.

But the next week, Fields was still the only executive with a red on his scorecard. Folks thought that the last meeting was just a bit of theater before Fields' inevitable termination. Only when they saw the *consistent* warm signals from Mulally on Frequency 2 did they realize it wasn't a trap. The following Thursday, the scorecards were "splattered with more red than a crime scene," Mulally would later recall. Now he knew why they were losing so much money! And with visibility, they could start solving problems. Mulally would describe this as the defining moment in the company's turnaround.

Though not as dramatic, here are a few other examples of leaders realigning reward signals with the performance and behavior they want to see more of:

Realignment: Rewards for raising the red flag. When he founded Roivant Sciences, a biotech firm, Vivek Ramaswamy had an epiphany: "While virtually all pharma companies say they encourage risk," he said, "in reality the failure of individual drug-development programs frequently results in career damage or even job loss for the research teams involved."[8] And yet "the reasons for failure frequently have less to do with the quality of the teams working on the programs and more to do with the underlying science. As a result, teams are perversely incentivized to protect and prolong dubious drug-development programs, diverting resources from more promising avenues of research." What's the alternative?

They rewarded teams for raising red flags about programs, so they could be halted. They used stock options to give everyone a stake in the firm's collective performance (rather than having a stake only in the success of their assigned program.) And, says Ramaswamy, "all members of research teams are promised new roles within the Roivant family of companies if their particular program or subsidiary does not succeed."

Realignment: Rewards for fire prevention, rather than firefighting. Katherine Kountze, CIO at Eversource, recognized the need to deliver customer value with processes that are more stable and sustainable. That would require changing up the signals broadcast on Frequency 2. "When you're changing culture, you've got to be careful about your reward signals and what behaviors you reinforce," she told us. "I don't want to see more great firefighting that isn't accompanied by addressing 'how do we solve the problem long-term?' I want my warm signals to reinforce the 'I'm going to make sure no other customer experiences this'-orientation rather than 'I'm simply going to make the customer happy right now.'"

Realignment: Recognition for innovative ideas. At Talen Energy, leaders wanted to solicit employees' input on ways to simplify processes and save money without compromising safety or reliability. But they recognized that in the past, they hadn't done a good job of managing employees' ideas and visibly taking action on them. So why would employees feel motivated to invest discretionary energy this go around? This time when they asked for suggestions, leaders made submission easy, promised a smarter approach for prioritizing and acting on ideas, and said: "Even if you've turned it in before, tell us again." This request was credible enough to produce 500 innovative ideas. Of course, just like in the past, leaders couldn't do everything. So Senior Vice President Tim Rausch and his team evaluated the ideas based on ease of implementation and return on investment. Based on those criteria, they listed the top ten ideas and the employees associated with each, so their leader and peers could recognize them. And then as each of these top ten ideas was executed, they celebrated, then put the next top ten in place. "And then when the CEO comes to the facility," Tim says, "he'll have lunch with the employees whose ideas were most recently implemented as a way of saying thanks for helping to shape the culture we're after." By more closely aligning warm signals with the behavior they want to see more, even more employees are now submitting innovations. "Meanwhile," Tim told us, "we've reduced our costs 22 percent in the past 11 months."

Realignment: Rewarding high performance (without spending lots of money). According to Christy Kenny, HR Director at PSEG Nuclear, leaders realized that the company's nuclear fleet was missing an opportunity with their high performers. They asked themselves: "Are we saying to the people most responsible for the positive trajectory in plant performance: We are paying attention to you and want to help to strategically manage your future here?" And their answer was "no." "And we knew that wouldn't work," Christy said. "That amounts to withholding a reward from performers who deserve it."

Plant leaders understood that change didn't require spending boatloads of money. But they did need to formalize the process. "Now we regularly identify the top 20 talents of the site and we assign each of them a leader / mentor," Christy said. "Then the Chief Nuclear Officer meets with each one to identify explicitly what he most appreciates about that performer, and to talk about her or his career path. This is a powerful reward that costs no money. And it's helped put in place a winning culture."

§§§§§

We've just covered this chapter's first coaching point: "Reward what you want to see more of." Now its corollary, and the other thing great leaders do to transmit strong and steady signals on Frequency 2: They understand and leverage the emotional algorithms that motivate their people. This is how they make their warm signals as effective as possible. We'll devote the rest of this chapter to this topic.

Signal Boost #2: Understand the emotional algorithms that motivate your people

In 2002, Daniel Kahneman won the Nobel Prize in economics. This was the first time the award went to someone who had never even taken an economics course. Kahneman had a background in psychology, which meant that—unlike most economists over the past three centuries—he was comfortable talking about feelings. Not *his* feelings, necessarily, but rather how emotions influence humans' in-the-moment calculations of economic utility.

Before proceeding, let's refresh your memory about that term, which you may recall from Economics 101: *Utility* refers to the value that individuals gain from a "good" experience. We make choices, according to the logic of economics, that we think will maximize our utility—taking into account our options and their relative tradeoffs.

Kahneman's big insight? "Utility cannot be divorced from emotion...A theory of choice that completely ignores feelings...leads to prescriptions that do not maximize the utility of outcomes as they are actually experienced."

Put more simply, if you're trying to predict human economic behavior—and you don't include emotions in your equation—your predictions will probably be way off. Emotions factor heavily into the algorithms that produce our trade-off decisions. We make them based on how we expect those choices will lead us to *feel*. This is obvious when we observe someone driving (or aspiring to drive) a Lexus rather than a Toyota-branded version of essentially the same vehicle. Or eating in exclusive restaurants. Or ordering new exercise equipment after watching an infomercial.

Indeed, the field of advertising is almost entirely predicated on the motivating power of emotions. Nonetheless, Kahneman's insights shook up the field of economics. He got his readers thinking differently.

Kahneman's insights can help leaders think differently, too.

Practical application for leaders. Maybe you don't think of it this way, but we can characterize the relationship between you and people who work for you as an ongoing series of economic transactions. Today, will your people give you their best attention and discretionary energy, which for them are finite resources? Or will they put that attention and energy into, say, scanning the waiver wire to shore up their fantasy football team, or sharing memes on social media, or watching baby elephant GIFs? And, in the coming months, will your high performers stick with you...or look for another job? As utility maximizers, they'll make those choices based on emotional algorithms.

When your people give you their best attention and discretionary energy, when they stick with you instead of pursuing another job that would pay more money, it's because of the way working for you makes them *feel*. Respected. Appreciated. Affiliated. Successful. Purposeful. Autonomous. Secure. Some combination of the preceding adjectives. Or maybe something else entirely.

An example: "Emotional compensation" at Gorilla Logic. Gorilla Logic provides web, mobile, and enterprise software development solutions for a growing number of U.S. companies. Gorilla is a tech firm very selective in its recruitment, hiring only the most talented applicants. Competitive pay helps attract A Players. But how do they hang on to them? What explains the company's very low turnover rates? According to Mario Merino, the managing director of the company's nearshoring operations in San Jose, Costa Rica, "emotional compensation" is the most important variable. For example, the company offers highly flexible work arrangements, provides yoga and mixed-martial arts classes several times per week (in addition to many other social and cultural activities). And there's beer in the break room refrigerator. But the most important element of emotional compensation, Merino told us, is brain candy: "We offer our gorillas [which is what the company calls its consultants] the most interesting and challenging puzzles they may ever see." Because Gorilla and its top talent have developed a reputation for solving challenging problems that competitors can't handle, they're able to charge a premium in the marketplace for their services—fueling explosive business growth and a steady supply of brain candy for the firm's consultants. It's a virtuous cycle.

Everyone is different. What works at Gorilla Logic might not work in your organization. That's one of the big challenges of being a leader—and in particular, transmitting effective "warm signals" on Frequency 2: Everyone's different. The utility or motivating value of any "warm signal" depends on its recipient's emotional make up and mindset. The idea that some people are motivated and others aren't is a myth. The reality is that everyone is motivated. They may not be motivated by the same things that motivate you or by what you think should motivate them. But everyone is most definitely motivated by something.

And this is a challenge that leaders have to embrace, says Beth M. Foley, Chief Communications Officer and Vice President of Corporate Communications for Edison International and Southern California Edison. "A significant obligation of being a leader is to learn what incentivizes and motivates your team members and co-workers," she says. "Everyone is inspired by different things. I enjoy figuring out what keeps them coming back every day and performing their best. Having one cookie-cutter approach simply does not work."

For example, sometimes the warm signal high performers covet most is more of your time and attention. For other high performers, the most effective way for you to reinforce their high performance is to stay the heck out of their way and provide more autonomy.

Sometimes, the very best performers simply don't want any attention. Talking about his attention-averse high performers, an executive told us: "They'll say, 'Please, I love my job, this company, my customers. Thank you for recognizing me—but I really don't want to stand up in front of people. Please don't make me.' What do you do? You tell people that Sharon was number one again for the fifth year in a row. But don't make her stand up. In fact, if she doesn't want to come to the ceremony, that's okay. With those kinds of things, you've got to know your people well enough that they're comfortable telling you if they're uncomfortable."

Everyone is different…but in some ways the same (usually). Everyone processes reward signals through their own unique emotional algorithms. And this makes it tough to be a leader and culture-shaper, since one of your jobs is to effectively align warm signals with the behavior and performance you want to see more of. The good news? There are six principles that apply to *most* of your people. Understanding these principles can help you broadcast stronger signals on Frequency 2.

1. It's all relative.
2. People are more sensitive to losses than gains.
3. Scarcity matters.
4. Timing matters.
5. For most, meaningful work is motivating.
6. Everyone appreciates being appreciated.

1. It's all relative.

What's the motivating value of a $10,000 year-end bonus? Well, it depends on three relative comparisons.

The first comparison is: How does the reward compare with what the recipient expects? As neuroscientists are learning, the dopamine neurons in our brains, which help us make decisions about what to keep doing or stop doing, respond not to rewards or their absence but to "deviations from expectations." What's more, violations of expectations trigger powerful emotional responses.[9] Thus, if you give the $10,000 year-end bonus to an employee who got a $5,000 bonus last year and has worked hard to improve his performance in the past 12 months, there's a good chance the bonus you just issued will positively violate expectations, and will help motivate him to continue improving his performance and give you discretionary effort. On the other hand, if you give the $10,000 bonus to an employee who got $25,000 last year, and if you neglect in advance to explain the difference, she's probably going to walk away. And that's why we say that just because something is very easy to measure—in this case, a $10,000 bonus measured in hard dollars—it doesn't mean the measurement is meaningful.

The second relative comparison is: What are other people getting? A $5,000 bonus will produce a stronger influence on the recipient if he knows that most of his peers received a bonus half that size. But, if he learns that some of his peers received $7,500 for what he perceives to be similar or inferior performances, the motivating power of that same $5,000 disappears, and he feels insulted.

Of course, perceptions of fairness come into play when we make social comparisons. In fact, it appears we're wired to make very sensitive calibrations about whether something is fair. According to researchers, we process "concepts of fairness…in the insular cortex, or insula, which is also the seat of emotional reactions."[10] This goes a long way toward explaining some of the things we repeatedly find in our culture research, specifically the high levels of resentment that employees feel when:

- *They perceive that the organization tolerates poor performers.* Across organizations, we find that employees are highly conscious of what leaders do about "dead weight." As one executive told us, "When we allow poor performers to stay, we hear about it in employee surveys," she says. "They see it as an injustice...and they're right."

- *They perceive that the organization actually rewards poor performers.* We use a 360° assessment to help leaders evaluate their current effectiveness across each of the Five Frequencies. For a majority of leaders, one of their five lowest-rated scores is "making sure high performers don't get stuck making up for low performers." When leaders load up high performers because they're unwilling to or incapable of holding low performers accountable, the high performers eventually tend to notice and resent it.

Some leaders respond to these findings by saying (if only to us): "The people who are ticked off [because they perceive that we tolerate poor performers] should just worry about themselves and the employment deal we cut specifically with them. Let us decide how to deal with the poor performers." This argument has some logical appeal. But not much else. As Kahneman says, you should never assume that reactions governed "by the emotion of the moment will be internally coherent or even reasonable by the cooler criteria of reflective reasoning."

Another concern that leaders sometimes voice is whether rewarding high performers demotivates the rest of team. Recent experiments have examined this and researchers have found "it is possible to recognize top performers and boost team performance at the same time. In fact…recognizing a single team member seems to have a positive and contagious effect on all the other members in the team." The caveat: the recognition has to be timely and fairly administered.[11]

The third relative comparison is: What do I already have? Another term you may recall from Economics 101 is *declining marginal utility*, which is the idea that the more of something an individual has, the less valuable having more of it will be to that individual.[12] Financial rewards tend to exhibit declining marginal utility, as illustrated in this example: Jane started out in the mail room making $25,000 per year. At that level of compensation, a $2,000 bonus probably carried a lot of motivating influence. However, after Jane worked her way up to CEO and was drawing a $750,000 base, $2,000 was "lunch money."

Formal recognition programs are also susceptible to declining marginal utility. For example, imagine an employee who, thanks to a peer noticing her extra effort, receives a certificate she can hang on the wall of her cubicle. She's pretty darn happy. The next time she gets one, she's still happy about it, but the second certificate doesn't pack the positive emotional punch of the first. The third time she gets it, it's even less valuable, though certainly not unappreciated. Of course, social comparison can change the experience. If the employee has four certificates hanging on her wall and no one else has more than one, this might compensate for the declining marginal utility.

This is one of the reasons we're big fans of using developmental experiences and exciting challenges as rewards for performers. The more unique or novel an experience, the less vulnerable it is to declining marginal utility. But you've got to be careful. As one Fortune 25 executive told us, too often "development opportunity" is just a code word for giving people more work. ("The reward for winning the pie-eating contest is…more pie!") For people to actually learn something, you need to have:

- A targeted outcome in mind.
- Some level of preparation to take on the opportunity.
- Some level of stretch or discomfort to encourage people to grow.
- Some time for reflection about what's happened.

"Without these things, people won't take anything away," the executive said. "While that sounds obvious, so much 'development activity' isn't characterized by any of these things!" Which means it's delusional to think you're really "rewarding what you want to see more of."

2. People are more sensitive to losses than gains.

Kahneman found that humans are about 2.5x more sensitive to losses than equivalent gains. For example, the pain of losing $100 isn't equal to the satisfaction of finding $100. The pain of that loss is more equivalent—to the extent that one can compare such things—to the joy of finding $200 to $250.

One of the practical implications of this is that lots of leaders are unintentionally administering negative consequences—often without even knowing it. Some examples:

- You tell a junior associate that you're going to hand him control of an important account. You come back two hours later and say, "Y'know, I changed my mind." You think the net effect is zero. In the real world, though, that up-and-comer feels 2.5x worse than if you'd never said a word.

- You decide to provide free snacks and caffeinated beverages for everyone staying late. A month later, you're surprised by how much it costs to provide the perk. Apparently, your people eat a lot of snacks. Lesson learned. Now there's an "honor box" for them to pay for their snacks. Why are they ticked about it? There were no snacks at all a month ago. Well, now you know.

So what are we saying? You can never change your mind? No. But if you know this principle, it might help you to avoid some choices that create unintended negative consequences.

3. Scarcity matters.

As Robert Cialdini observed in his classic treatise, *Influence*, "[O]pportunities seem more valuable to us when their availability is limited." He describes an experiment conducted by Stephen Worchel in which participants were handed a cookie from a jar and asked to taste it and rate its desirability. Half the participants received their cookie from a jar with nine others; the other half received an identical cookie from a jar that contained just two. "As we might expect from the scarcity principle," Cialdini says, "when the cookie was one of the only two available, it was rated more favorably than when it was one of ten." Respondents reported higher levels of desire and attributed greater value to "the cookie in short supply."

Thinking about all the ways you can provide warm signals, which are your "cookies in short supply?"

The list might include exciting assignments, prizes (money, vacations, etc.), operational resources (budget, headcount, etc.), or developmental resources (arranging for a mentor, hiring an executive coach).

For many leaders, another highly scarce resource is their time and attention. Investing time with your A Players sends the message, "The more you perform, the more I'm interested in what you're doing, and the more time I'll spend with you." At the same time, you must be careful about the amount of time you spend with the people who are the biggest pains in the neck. They may be the ones who are constantly asking for it and requiring it, but focusing too much time on them actually provides warm signals for those who screw up.

According to our colleague, Leadership Circle CEO Bill Adams, "I'm observing that a lot of up-and-comers are choosing between job offers less on the basis of dollars and more on the basis of how much time and attention they are going to get from their leader. For example, I talked recently with a guy who is considering a senior role. He's trying to determine if his prospective leader will take the time to give him positive and negative feedback to ensure that his direction is clear. That's his choice point."

4. Timing matters.

The longer it takes to deliver a warm signal in response to a great performance, the less likely it is to have motivating impact. By bringing positive consequences closer, you more effectively reinforce the behavior you want to see more of.

A colleague learned from her leadership experience, the wisdom of adopting "a spur-of-the-moment approach" to warm signals. "By that," she says, "I mean connecting with people directly, looking them in the eye, shaking their hand and saying, 'That was awesome. Great job.' You stop right there and engage them in a conversation to reinforce something exemplary." What's important is (1) timeliness—as soon as you are aware of the exemplary performance—and (2) specificity—telling people exactly what they did that made the difference.

A financial services firm helped make their culture a source of competitive advantage, and attracted and retained A Players as a result, by keeping a carrot constantly in front of employees: "Look at Wall Street's approach to retention," the CEO told us. "They always lose their employees at the beginning of every year. It's because of the poor payout schedule. Employees receive an annual bonus on January 15 or February 15, and right after they get it, they walk out the door."

"But here, we structure our calendar to keep high-performing employees: In January, you don't want to leave because that's when you're getting paid on December's business, which typically includes your highest commissions. In February, you don't want to leave because you have the Leader's Club trip, which the top people go to, and it's such a great location. At this point, you may say, 'I'm just going to wait until after the trip, then I'll leave.' But then, in March, you don't want to leave because your 401k matching contribution hits. And then April, May, and June fly by, and there are cash retention payouts in July. No one's going to leave before then, or they'd be walking away from $50,000. By fall, you've got all this momentum, and you're not going to leave because it just wouldn't make any sense to walk away from the money."

Manage the Ending

When you give someone a pain-in-the-butt assignment, manage how it ends. It may significantly increase the odds they're willing to take on the next such assignment. A recent study examined the intensity of pain reported by two groups of people who underwent colonoscopies.

> For half the patients, the instrument was not immediately removed when the clinical examination ended. Instead, the physician waited for about a minute, leaving the instrument stationary. The experience during the extra period was uncomfortable, but the procedure guaranteed that the colonoscopy never ended in severe pain.[13]

In short, the people whose colonoscopies lasted longer but ended less painfully reported much more favorable attitudes and, by extension, were less resistant to signing up for another such experience in the future. How can leaders apply the *Comfortable Colonoscopy Completion Principle* at the end of a painful assignment they've given to one or more of their star performers?

- First, manage the ending. They'll remember what's most recent. Don't just let the project end. Control the ending with something (or ideally a number of things that are) positive. Celebrate successes and show appreciation with a day off...team dinner...senior leaders acknowledging the team...rewards and recognition for the team as a whole and for individuals on the team, etc. Whatever it is, make it meaningful and substantial—because a quick handshake from the CEO doesn't erase 18 months of pain. Another way to end on at least a neutral, if not positive, note is to conduct a lessons learned session, even if the project was messy. It can help people feel smart, useful, and acknowledged—and more confident that whatever the organization stumbled on this time isn't going to trip them up in the next go 'round.

- Second, manage what comes after the ending. Why? Because no one wants to endure one colonoscopy after another. How? Immediately following a tough project...

  ✓ Give your high-potentials choices about their next assignment (give them the chance to do something they're excited and passionate about).

  ✓ Allow time for them to reenergize (with downtime, a less-demanding project, etc.).

  ✓ Support developmental activities (classes, courses, conferences, job rotations, etc.).

5. For most, meaningful work is motivating.

There's an old story about a traveler in Medieval times who comes across a stonecutter. The stonecutter is whacking at a stone. He's unfocused and looks miserable. "What are you doing?" the traveler asks. "What does it look like I'm doing?" the stonecutter replies, incredulous. "I'm cutting stones and this job stinks."

The traveler continues until he sees another stonecutter. This stonecutter is whacking away at his stone with extra energy and an enthusiastic smile on his face. "What are you doing?" the traveler asks. "I'm building a cathedral," the happy stonecutter replies.

The moral of the story? Meaningful work can be its own reward. In the real world, two things are typically required for work to be meaningful and self-rewarding. First, there must be line of sight to a motivating purpose or righteous cause. For the second stonecutter, that righteous cause is sharing in the glory of building a cathedral. The first stonecutter only understood the drudgery of monotonous manual labor and couldn't see the big picture.

Real world examples? For one of our pharmaceutical clients, that driving purpose is "getting more of our medicines to more patients faster." For the employees of the City of Detroit under Mayor Mike Duggan's leadership, the righteous cause is a Detroit where the population is growing, and every Detroiter has an opportunity to participate in that growth.

But line of sight to a motivating purpose is only half the equation. In the real world, the second stonecutter is giving that kind of discretionary energy only if he feels empowered to problem-solve and implement continuous improvement efforts.

If he is, great things can happen. And that's true even if he's represented by Local 23 of the Stonecutters union. In fact, our statistical modeling of what drives employee performance and behavior shows time and again that empowerment and line of sight are at least as important to represented employees as they are to non-represented employees. Sometimes more so.

This is underscored in a story that American Electric Power CEO Nick Akins shared:

> We launched a continuous improvement activity where we brought field-level employees together to focus on changes

that would drive efficiency—and do so in a way that was open and collaborative. I went to almost all of the team report-outs. And at least twice I watched employees who'd been on the job for 35 years on the verge of tears because they'd never been asked to participate in something like this before. Many said they were about to retire because they "just couldn't take it anymore." Now because of their engagement in problem solving and practical continuous improvement, it feels like a different company to them. It is a different company.

6. Everyone appreciates being appreciated.

Many leaders underappreciate and underutilize simple expressions of gratitude as a reinforcing warm signal.

Here are four reasons that should change:

First, saying "thanks" doesn't cost you money and requires hardly any time. But it does require that you pay attention.

Second, research shows that in many organizations there's a sizable recognition gap. For example, a recent TinyPulse survey[14] across the finance industry found that just 21 percent of employees felt appropriately recognized. Some illustrative comments from the other 79 percent:

- "I do great work all year, very rarely do I even get told I'm doing a good job. Come review time all is forgotten and I'm only reminded about a few things I could have done better. Maybe it's to make me grow, maybe it's because you know it'll keep me working hard to try to please someone, either way it's depressing."

- "I am not looking for a pat on the back every time I do something for a co-worker or a customer. But I think my hard work has been ignored. I have gone above and beyond in many ways and never recognized for it."

- "One or two people may say 'Good Job' but for the most part, I feel as if the perception of me is that I am a waste of cubicle space."

Third, research shows that when you reinforce strong and improving performances with timely, specific appreciation, it leads to more of the same, which strengthens business performance. (Obviously.)[15]

Fourth, and perhaps less obviously, simple warm signals can be as rewarding for the giver as the getter. According to Beth M. Foley, whom you met earlier in the chapter:

> Never underestimate the power of a handwritten, personal note. Sometimes it is a team member, colleague or even a board member. I like to share with them how they positively impacted our customers or co-workers, or how I believe they were living our values. Other times it's people in my personal life—the SoulCycle instructor who helped me through something more than she knows, the team member at a hotel who epitomized his company's brand, or the airline attendant who treated another passenger with exceedingly tremendous compassion. (And trust me, those folks don't get a lot of compliments.) From a personal perspective, writing them is a fulfilling and positive way to wind down a work week. I confess, I get a natural high from each and every missive I scribe, and if my words support someone moving toward his or her goals, that is a bonus.

Signal Boost Summary

Want to turn your culture into a source of competitive advantage? Use these Frequency 2 Signal Boosts:

- **Reward what you want to see more of:** If you want your people to do some particular thing, you'd better line up your "warm signals" with that performance or behavior. Remember "It's folly to reward A while hoping for B."[16]

- **Understand—and leverage—the emotional algorithms that motivate your people.**

  1. It's all relative—to what's expected, to what others get, and what the recipient already has.

  2. People are more sensitive to losses than gains.

  3. Scarcity matters (making rewards more meaningful).

  4. Timing matters—so bring positive consequences closer.

  5. For most, meaningful work is motivating.

  6. Everyone appreciates being appreciated.

CHAPTER 3

FREQUENCY 3: WHAT YOU TOLERATE (OR DON'T)

FIVE FREQUENCIES

Frequency 3: What you tolerate (or don't)

This chapter covers six signal boosts for turning culture into competitive advantage

- **Remember: You're defined by what you tolerate**
- **Set it and forget it**
- **Align your cold signals**
- **Lose your excuses**
- **Equip people for Moments of Truth**
- **Be smart about what you *do* tolerate**

We're going to tell you here about a well-known leader who is successfully shifting the culture of the organization he leads with strong and steady signals across Five Frequencies. *Forbes* says he has already taken that "culture from…one of 'institutional self-preservation' back to its core mission" and in the process, "transform[ed] a 2,000-year-old brand."[1]

And then we'll tell you why, instead of featuring him in the book's introduction, we are instead using his story as a cautionary tale for our examination of Frequency 3.

We're talking about Pope Francis.

Frequency 1: Leaders' decisions and actions

For Pope Francis, conscious culture-shaping literally started on day one. Shortly after the Congress of Cardinals elected him pontiff, Pope Francis realized he'd forgotten to check out of his hotel room. So, he got on a bus with some other cardinals, went back to the hotel, and took care of the bill himself. Presumably the papacy comes with plenty of perks—and lots of people could have taken care of this for him. But he chose to do it himself.

When asked about this by the media, the Pope said he wanted to set an example for the cardinals and the bishops regarding how he would like to see them act: With humility, responsibility, and accountability.

Frequency 2: What leaders reward and recognize

Whether they know it or not, leaders send reward signals as a result of who they spend time with. So, who does Pope Francis spend time with? The poor, the sick, and the homeless, among others. While each of these acts is sincere and valuable in its own right, the Pope is also sending signals that shape culture. His goal, almost certainly, is to re-center and align the organization with its core mission.

Frequency 3: What leaders tolerate (or don't)

Very shortly into his tenure, Pope Francis suspended the "Bishop of Bling," who had spent millions of dollars on home renovations—expenditures inconsistent with the mission of the Catholic Church as the Pope sees it. Since then, the Pope's also sacked four of the five cardinals directing the scandal-tainted Vatican Bank.

Frequency 4: How leaders show up informally

The Pope has mastered this frequency as well. Culture-shaping signals include posing for selfies with teenagers and eating in the Vatican cafeteria. The way he shows up builds trust and affiliation.

Frequency 5: Leaders' formal communications.

The Pope's strong and steady signals across the first four frequencies compel people to tune into the fifth. Crowds in Saint Peter's Square are up four-fold since the beginning of his papacy. In some parts of the world, church attendance is up 20 percent. In other words, with strong and steady signals on Five Frequencies, he's compelling people to do things they wouldn't have done otherwise. He's tapping into discretionary energy.

Imagine the transformative impact on business results *you* could produce if you unleashed a 20 percent increase in discretionary energy from your employees.

§§§§

So what's the problem?

Let's start with the explosive allegations of retired Vatican ambassador, Archbishop Carlo Maria Vigano. In an 11-page letter, Vigano accused the Pope of covering up for years the sexual misconduct of Theodore McCarrick, the former archbishop of Washington, D.C., who was credibly accused of sexual abuse of a minor, among other things.

Vigano didn't provide evidence to substantiate his claims. And as one news source noted, "The known fact is that when credible allegations recently surfaced that McCarrick had abused a minor, it was Pope Francis who elicited his resignation as cardinal — an extremely rare occurrence in the Catholic Church."[2]

Moreover, Vigano is a conservative traditionalist and has been critical of the Pope's progressivism. So perhaps his allegations are politically motivated.

But even if politics motivated Vigano to speak, it doesn't necessarily mean his charges aren't accurate. And the Pope's response to the charges—he told reporters, "make your own judgment. ... I believe the [Vigano] document speaks for itself"—didn't exactly constitute the fierce denial we expected.

So, did the Pope cover up for McCarrick? We hope not. We'd like to think not. We've been big fans (even though just one of us is Catholic.) But are we so confident in his innocence that we're comfortable showcasing him as an exemplar? Not at this moment.

Regardless of how this plays out, here's the point we want to make: **Leaders are ultimately defined by what they tolerate**—regardless of the strength and steadiness of their signals across the other frequencies. That's true for Pope Francis and that's true for you, too. Remembering that is this chapter's **Signal Boost #1**.

The rest of the chapter highlights five others.

Signal Boost #2: Set it and forget it

According to Andrew Fastow, the Enron CFO who spent more than five years in federal prison for fraud, "Employees will see through empty rhetoric and will emulate the nature of top-management decision making...A robust 'code of conduct' can be emasculated by one action of the CEO or CFO."[3]

Just one action. So consistency is key. Fastow learned the hard way. But that's something Richard Smith recognized all along. Prior to his recent retirement, Smith led Realogy, a $6 billion real estate and relocation services company. With Smith as CEO, Realogy was recognized six years in a row as one of the World's Most Ethical Companies by the Ethisphere Institute. A few months before Richard turned over the reins, we asked him what earning "most ethical" honors required.

"It starts with me," he said. "I hold myself to very high personal and professional standards every day and I expect others to do the same thing. I learned a long time ago that all leaders are on display every single day, both in their professional and personal lives."

Personal lives?

Yep. Given the nature of communication today, Smith believes that it's often very difficult to distinguish between your personal life and your corporate life. And that everything you do reflects directly on you, your family, and your company. "And to pretend different is a fallacy," he says. "If what you're about to do isn't something you want on the front page of *The Wall Street Journal* or you can't justify it to your mom, it's a bad idea."

Realogy's reputation as a highly ethical company is a source of competitive advantage. It helps the company attract and retain A Players. But it's far more than that. The company's "set it and forget it" approach to boundary-setting helps the organization lead and govern more efficiently.

How so?

"We make it very clear to you, if you cross the line, I don't care how productive you are or how valuable you are. If you have an illicit affair, or fudge an expense report, or play favorites, you're going to exit Realogy. Yesterday I was at a Business Review of one of our companies that's grown dramatically through acquisitions. At one of the companies they'd acquired, there was an improper romantic relationship between a manager and a lower-level employee. In the Review, there was a brief description of how the situation was handled.

But no deliberation was necessary. Everybody in the room knew exactly what position the company was going to take. I didn't have to say a word. There was no uncertainty."

And according to Richard, it's a tremendous source of business value when people know and understand exactly what the rules are, and they know exactly how the company's going to react in a given set of circumstances. Does he believe it's difficult to achieve? Yes… "but it's fantastic when you do."

Signal Boost #3: Align your cold signals

In the last chapter, which focused on Frequency 2, we emphasized the importance of lining up your warm signals with the behavior and performance you want to see more of. Because you're going to get more of what's rewarded and recognized. The flipside is also true: It's important to line up your cold signals with the behavior and performance you *don't* want to see any more of. You will almost always get more of what you tolerate.

There are two kinds of cold signals: Those focused on course correction and those focused primarily on punishment (in pursuit of justice and deterrence).

Course Correction. Course correction is about getting people pointed in the right direction. It's about coaching and feedback to improve performance. It's about intervention, boundary-setting, and consequences, with the goal of changing behavior and elevating performance.

Mike Rawlings, formerly president of Pizza Hut and currently the mayor of Dallas, was the city's Homeless Czar when he told us this story some years back:

> One of my strategies was to create the MetroDallas Homeless Alliance, an independent organization that could work across government and organizational boundaries. So I went out and hired a CEO, someone who was familiar with working with government and with the nonprofit sector. Very bright guy with a good heart. But he had never worked with someone like me.
>
> Our different backgrounds showed when we created objectives for the year. He started with a laundry list and with the mindset that the thicker the document is, the better it is. I wrote his objectives on a cocktail napkin—four or five big ones.
>
> At the end of the year, we sat down to evaluate his performance. First, I let him grade himself. And then I graded him. One of his objectives was a plan for permanent housing for the homeless. Very complex to do. But we had put it into his objectives and set a deadline for the end of the year. It really needed to be done. It wasn't. Another objective: I asked for a CFO to be hired. At the end of the year, it wasn't done. There were a lot of reasons why these things weren't done, but they weren't done. As a result, he did not get his full bonus. He wasn't happy.
>
> So going into what is now our second year, we still had unfinished objectives from the year before, plus a new set of objectives. This year, coming out of the gate, he jumped all over the objectives and took them very, very seriously. Permanent, supportive housing plan? Almost done. CFO?

Hired. And the year's not over. Just about everything he has to do this year has been done and done well.

Once he realized that this was not government bureaucracy, that I was serious, and that there were real consequences for non-performance, he's been great.

It's a good example of aligning cold signals to lift performance. But to be clear: There's no reason to wait for an annual performance review to transmit them. That's like a football coach waiting until the end of the season to review game film with the team.

Waiting to deliver cold signals doesn't make any sense at all to Dr. Allen Weiss. When he was CEO of NCH Healthcare, he told us why this bothered him:

> I expect our physicians to be collegial, positive, cooperative and communicative. When I hear about bad behavior, I'll ask: "Did you call him out?" The answer is often, "No, because he's been like that for 15 years." Well, if we've let it slide for 15 years, then we have inadvertently trained physicians to not change.

The previous day, he'd spotted a surgeon wearing the required white coat but jeans and sandals underneath. Weiss stopped him: "Please put on some socks, buddy. You're setting an example for the residents." As Weiss told us later, "That's all it takes. If you don't wait 15 years to enforce standards, it often requires only a very small cold signal to bring performance in line with expectations."

Weiss also conceded that "there are some old curmudgeons who don't want to change. They think, 'I'm going to retire in five years. I *can't* change.' Well, that's five bad years for our patients and our co-workers—so we've had to part ways with some physicians who 'can't change.'"

But the truth is: Most people appreciate course correction. Leadership guru Marshall Goldsmith counsels senior leaders that their direct reports want "regular 'reality checks' to make sure that they are heading in the right direction." But it doesn't have to be a time-consuming process. The "frequency of interaction is often more important than the duration of interaction," Goldsmith says.[4]

And even if they don't admit it, most people welcome boundaries. A friend shared this experience early in his career working for a senior diplomat in Geneva: The diplomat, who had 400 reports, had a very casual way of operating. His assistant, who was French, had little respect for him, and she showed it.

She started taking longer and longer coffee breaks. From 15 minutes…to 20, 25, 30 minutes… until she got up to an hour. Finally, this very seasoned diplomat and manager had enough. He said, "I need you back in the office. I need you to attend to the work we pay you to do, and you cannot take these very long coffee breaks. I need you here. I expect you to be here." She promptly related the story to her colleagues, adding: "Finally, he is acting like a real boss."

Punitive action. When leaders are effective at course correction, there's far less need for the second type of cold signal: punitive action aimed at delivering justice and deterring anyone else from exhibiting the same behavior. Punitive action usually means termination, but sometimes organizations try to make do with lighter versions.

For example, Riot Games, a 1,700-employee videogame maker based in Southern California, recently implemented a two-month suspension for its COO, Scott Gelb. Gelb reportedly farted in employees' faces, humped them, and hit their testicles "as a part of what was described as a running workplace gag."[5] The punitive cold signal is part of a larger, 16-month cultural transformation the company has undertaken.

As of this writing, Riot's 16-month transformation strategy has not run its course. So the jury is still out on whether suspension (as opposed to termination) for Gelb is a sufficient cold signal to drive meaningful and sustainable culture change. (Call us old-fashioned, and not that we were asked, but for the record: We think the farting, humping, and testicle-hitting stuff is Rubicon-crossing behavior from which there is no coming back.)

But in Gelb's defense, it's possible he never got any course-correcting cold signals until the suspension came down. Maybe the CEO never told him his behavior had to change. Maybe he started out doing less egregious things and continued getting more obnoxious because there were no apparent boundaries.

Signal Boost #4: Lose your excuses

Humans are awesome at excuse-making. But it's not our fault. We're wired for it. Quick-triggered defensiveness proved to be an evolutionary advantage for our primitive ancestors. When they confronted threats (like coming around a corner and facing a sabertooth tiger), defensive instincts helped them survive long enough to become our primitive ancestors—by getting a head start on their less-survival-savvy peers, who were eaten).

As humans evolved, we harnessed that rapid-deploy defensiveness not just for protecting our bodies, but also our egos and identities. That's where excuse-making came from: According to social scientists,[6] we invented it to protect the ego through self-serving explanations that help to avoid personal responsibility.

By extension, excuse-making proves very useful to help leaders justify why they don't need to broadcast strong and steady signals on Frequency 3. But, of course, this has a lot of negative downstream consequences...for culture...and for business performance. That's why the next Signal Boost in this chapter is: Lose your excuses.

As our friend Gregg Baron says, "Awareness precedes choice. And choice precedes change." So if you know the most common excuses leaders use to avoid their responsibilities on this frequency, you'll have the self-awareness that's a prerequisite for deciding not to deploy them. Here are the Frequency 3-related excuses we see most often.

Excuse #1: "I don't want to feel bad." When Tanya was very young, she and her family moved to Arusha, Tanzania. Behind the house was a garden, where Tanya's father, Roger, raised vegetables. A local gardener tended the garden from Monday to Saturday. On Sundays, when the gardener wasn't there, monkeys stole from the garden. Roger asked one of his friends for advice. "No problem," he said. "I'll bring my gun over and shoot one of them. It will scare the others away."

Yikes. Roger didn't like that idea at all. He felt really bad about the prospect of shooting a monkey.

"Yes, but that's what you've got to do," his neighbors advised.

When Roger insisted there must be an alternative, they humored him. Someone suggested that they trap one of the monkeys and hang a cowbell on him. "Maybe the noise will frighten away all the other monkeys." So Roger found someone who was very clever to design a trap and hired a carpenter to build it. The next Sunday they loaded it with bait and very quickly trapped a monkey. And then, with a bunch of help, they put a cowbell around the monkey's neck.

It didn't work: The vegetable thievery continued. "And it was annoying," Roger recalls, "because we could hear this monkey running around with a cowbell around his neck, and it didn't seem to bother any of the other monkeys. In fact, I suspect it became a source of prestige for him!"

Again, one of Roger's friends offered to come and shoot one of the monkeys, but again Roger resisted. Continuing to humor him, another neighbor theorized that if they trapped a monkey and painted him white, the others would think they were seeing a ghost, and it would scare them all away. So Roger trapped another monkey and painted him white with a good oil-based paint. Same outcome: The other monkeys were intrigued, not scared.

The next Sunday, Roger's friend—the one with the gun—came over. Together they crouched in the garden. When a monkey showed up in the branches above, Roger's friend took aim, fired one shot, and the dead monkey dropped to the ground. They never had another problem with monkeys stealing from their garden.

The good news for you—and we're very certain about this—is that shifting culture for competitive advantage will never require that you shoot a monkey. Or physically harm them or any other primates, including those of our species. This we guarantee.

At the same time, we are also certain that transmitting strong and steady signals on Frequency 3 *will* at least occasionally require you to do things that injure other people's egos and feelings. This, in turn, could make you feel bad. Instead of confronting the problem, you may be tempted, metaphorically speaking, to tie a cowbell around its neck.

That's what happened with a CEO with whom we worked with a few years ago. He was brought in to transform the organization's performance. That would require new investments, new talent, new processes—and, last but not least—a new culture. He brought us in to help with that last variable.

As part of the engagement, everyone on the senior team completed a Five Frequencies® 360° Leadership Profile. The CEO got relatively high scores from his raters on four of the five frequencies, everything but Frequency 3. His three lowest ratings:

- Identifying and addressing small issues and gaps before they turn into bigger problems.
- Delivering negative consequences consistently and fairly.
- Effectively addressing under-performance or bad behavior.

In the debrief, he committed to work on boosting his signal strength in these areas. A big opportunity came soon enough.

We were still early in the transformation process when it became clear that a new member of the senior team was a bad hire. He yelled at his colleagues. He frightened his employees. He told demonstrable lies. Independently, multiple members of the senior team went to the CEO and said, "You've got to do something. He's a cancer on the team. This is a big distraction and it's hurting performance."

When the CEO asked for our advice, we said, "Remember, you're defined by what you tolerate. You know what to do."

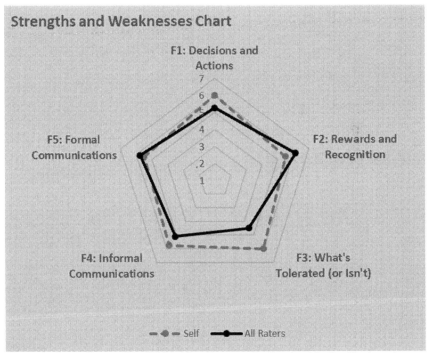

Figure 1: According to this CEO's Five Frequencies Leadership Profile, he tolerates too much

And the CEO *did* know. But he didn't fire the guy.

Why? The CEO felt bad. The team member had moved his family from two states away. He had a son in college. Getting fired would crush this person, who at times could be very likable.

And maybe, the CEO thought, he hadn't sufficiently communicated his expectations about how he wanted his team members to show up as leaders. And so the CEO had with this team member a stern conversation. Or at least that's how the CEO described it.

By some accounts, the team member's behavior improved for a week or so. By other accounts, he sustained his good behavior even longer. But by the six-week mark, he was back to his old ways.

The team member had had his chance. So the CEO brought him in to fire him. But the team member was so freaked out, and so apparently remorseful, and so committed to make amends, that the CEO gave him One. More. Chance.

The relapse started about three weeks later. And the CEO finally fired him about five weeks after that. (The team member was very surprised.)

Meanwhile, dozens of people were distracted and demoralized, which undermined an already-challenging-enough business and cultural transformation. And the process of finding an A Player-replacement had been needlessly delayed.

Now this CEO *really* had a reason to feel bad.

This CEO was hardly the first leader to the let the "I don't want to feel bad" excuse get in the way of transmitting necessary cold signals. The two-fifths of all leaders surveyed in a recent Harris Poll—who said that they're uncomfortable confronting poor performance when they think the employee might respond negatively to the feedback—are all likely culprits.[7]

But many other leaders don't let that get in the way. They recognize that being a good leader and making sure everyone likes you are not the same thing. That kindness doesn't equal weakness. "I want people to be approachable. I want to listen. But you still have to hold people accountable." That's according to Bob Walton, an executive with whom we've worked in a couple of different companies. One of his direct reports was very senior, very experienced. They had an absolutely collegial relationship. On one occasion, to help Bob meet his commitments to the board, the report promised an analysis by the end of the following Monday. When it didn't arrive, Bob didn't say, "Oh well, I know you had a difficult week." Instead, Bob asked: "What's going on? Do you need help? Do you not have resources? Did something come up that I'm not aware of?"

"I want to understand the problem," Bob said. "But I also want to signal that a commitment is a commitment."

Similarly, other leaders, recognize that leaning into unpleasant conversations can, in fact, turn out to be the compassionate thing to do. One of them is like Allie Shobe, a talent and organization executive at Accenture. Allie recalls psyching herself up to talk to one project manager. This project manager had interviewed well but once on the job her demeanor had changed. She came across as meek and unfocused. Then Allie learned that the project manager's husband was dying of cancer. She was the primary breadwinner. No wonder she was unfocused! She was stressed out and doing her best.

So Allie paired her up with a colleague to help make sure the work got done. But that made the project manager feel defensive. She resisted that option.

"In the next conversation, the conversation I wasn't looking forward to," Allie says, "we needed to talk about the fact that the required work wasn't getting done. I approached the conversation with a sense of dread. But it turned out to be one of the best I've ever had with anyone."

Allie told the project manager she was doing an amazing job given what she was dealing with. But Allie also spoke to her honestly about the gap between what the job required and how she was showing up.

"I didn't blame her," Allie recalls. "But I needed her support for a solution to close the gap. I asked her what story she was telling herself about the situation. It turns out she was blaming herself and feeling terrible and trying to prove something by staying on the job. Once she'd said it out loud, she realized it didn't make sense. The conversation concluded with her decision to leave the role. She said later that stepping away and spending more time with her husband was the best thing she'd ever done."

For Allie it reinforced her belief that having a candid (but empathetic) conversation about performance—instead of dancing around the issue—is the compassionate thing to do for people you care about.

Excuse #2: "I'm held hostage. I have no choice." Isaac Hanna is a Michigan-based entrepreneur. He is the founder of Wireless Giant—a retailer with over 60 locations, as well as several other successful companies. Isaac's family immigrated to the U.S. from Iraq in the 1970s.

On November 2, 1980, he was 16 years old and he worked at the family's market. That night he gave his father a recap of his day and then went to take a shower. By the time he returned, his father had died of a brain aneurysm.

Three days after the burial, Isaac's mother handed him the keys to market and said, "You're going to have to run it." He was in 11th grade.

But Isaac remained committed to become the first person in his family to graduate from high school. So he went to school during the day and to work immediately afterward. The one employee who wasn't family was the butcher. His name was George and he was a gambler. George would frequently come to Isaac and say, "Isaac, I need a loan. Please give me next week's pay in advance." And Isaac would do it because he didn't know how to cut meat and didn't want George to quit.

"But I didn't like feeling held hostage to George's bad habits," Isaac recalls, "so I sent my brother to help George so he could learn how to cut meat." There was a lot to learn. "In those days," Isaac said, "cattle didn't arrive cut up in boxes. Cattle came as cattle, on a hook. But a week later my brother assured me he was beginning to learn the job."

The next time George came to Isaac and asked for money Isaac said, "George, you'll have to find it somewhere else. I've already given you three weeks advance."

"Then I'll quit," George said. He took off his butcher's apron, threw it on the floor, and stormed out. That was a Friday. Weekends were the market's busiest times. Isaac's brother wasn't really ready yet to be a butcher, but somehow, they survived until Monday. That's when George came in and asked: "Who cut the meat?" Isaac said, "We did."

"The truth was," admitted Isaac, "we needed a real butcher. So I rehired him—but he never asked for money again. Ever."

§§§§

As an 11th grader, Isaac had the courage not to deploy the "I'm a hostage and have no choice" excuse. But many, much-more-seasoned leaders today lack that courage. When leaders use this excuse, what they're typically trying to avoid is short-term pain. Some examples:

- "Dealing with this person is going to take time that I don't have." (Sometimes followed by: "I'll just give the job to one of my high performers.")
- "I'd like to 'performance manage' this person out of here but I don't want to deal with HR."
- "I've already had a tough day. Giving someone tough feedback will just make it even more unpleasant."

We can empathize. Nobody likes short-term pain. But, for heaven's sake, make tough leadership decisions based on calculations of costs and benefits with a time horizon longer than one week. Because if you calculate your cost-benefit analysis based on what gets the best ROI by close of business, you'll always have an excuse to avoid the short-term pain. By tolerating bad behavior today, you're taking the benefits now and pushing out the costs. But they don't go away. They compound. This is why foreign policy analysts advise against "negotiating with terrorists." In the long run, it legitimates bad actors and actions—and undermines the good ones.[8]

If, instead, you take into account the downstream costs of tolerating bad behavior and calculate ROI on your leadership choices even six months out, you'll probably determine it's entirely irrational to be held hostage to gambling butchers or anyone else. (Like we said in Chapter 1, great culture-shapers are "long-term greedy.")

Excuse #3: "I can't hold *this* person accountable." Brad Mills is a fellow Philadelphian, and a successful real estate broker and consultant. But a few decades ago, in the mid-1980s, he was the young Company Commander of 330 Marines.

He had in his command a company staff sergeant who'd spent a lot of time in Vietnam and earned a Silver Star for his service there.

The company needed to produce a training plan for the coming year. It was a big document. An important document. Brad asked the staff sergeant to produce it. Brad provided a deadline that would give himself a few days to review and revise it before he had to take it up the chain of command.

On the date of the internal deadline, Brad went to the staff sergeant and asked, "Where's the plan?"

"Oh, sorry, sorry," he said. "I don't have it. I'll have it for you tomorrow." And he walked out.

Brad's first sergeant, who'd observed the conversation, turned to Brad and said, "But you need that today."

Brad mumbled something about not being able to push him too hard, because, after all, "This guy's highly decorated."

The first sergeant let him finish and then said: "Let me ask you a question, sir. When is he going to have to start earning a living again?"

Brad was confused. "What do you mean?"

"When do you think he got his medals in Vietnam? 1968? That was nearly 20 years ago," the first sergeant replied. "He's had a good run on those. But if you tell him he doesn't have to do another thing, he's just going to collect a paycheck every two weeks until he retires."

Brad turned and walked into the staff sergeant's office and said, "You know what? I really need this by the end of the day."

"Yes, sir," the staff sergeant replied. He turned in the plan that day and Brad never had another problem with him. Reflecting on the experience, Brad feels grateful to the first sergeant for "waking me up."

When you deploy the "I can't hold *this* person accountable" excuse, sometimes the wake-up call is far more painful than Brad's was.

Randy Gier, formerly the chief consumer officer at Dr. Pepper/Snapple, once told us about a tough lesson he learned when he tolerated some bad behavior. Why'd he do it? Because the guy was getting results.

"What's worse," Randy said, "is that I promoted him!"

Why elevate him? "I thought I could manage it. I thought: We'll promote him, and then we'll talk to him, and we'll tell him that his negative behavior is not going to work anymore: 'Now that you're promoted, you're going to have to operate differently.' And guess what? All the employee heard was, 'I got promoted. I must be very good, so I'm going to do more of it.'"

Randy continued: "And then you end up needing a bigger two-by-four later on to hit him on the side of the head and say, 'Did you not hear me?' Or you end up firing him. Only now, you've got someone you just invested in and promoted. And you've sent all the wrong messages to your organization. They think, 'They promoted that guy? Don't they get that he's a jerk?' They don't believe you couldn't see it, since everyone else does." Needless to say, culture takes a big hit.

In fact, culture takes a big hit anytime employees perceive that standards and consequences are applied inconsistently or that their leaders play favorites. It's crazy-making and demoralizing. The "I can't hold *this* person accountable" excuse is one of the worst.

That's why culture-savvy leaders never use it. Like a former executive at Lincoln Financial with whom we worked. Some years ago, at a national sales conference, one of the top people made an inappropriate, off-color remark at the podium. "So we fired him," the executive said. "He was shocked. He thought, 'I'm the top guy. They can't fire me.' But we did." Shortly after that, another top performer was caught cheating on his expenses. "And he was gone, too," the executive said. "If you just say, 'Don't say inappropriate things' and

'Don't cheat' but don't do anything about it, no one will listen. The trick is, you have to follow through." Even when the offender is otherwise a high performer.

Excuse #4: "This is just a small thing." Before a NATO summit in 2017, French President Emmanuel Macron and U.S. President Trump met before a press gathering. Cameras captured them smiling, intently looking each other in the eyes, and, for an uncomfortable length of time, gripping hands so tightly their knuckles turned white. Neither was willing to be out-handshaked by the other. Macron later said that he wanted to "show he would not make small concessions, not even symbolic ones."[9]

That's one way to summarize what's called "broken windows theory."[10] Guided by this theory, New York City Commissioner William Bratton led a successful, if controversial, effort to significantly reduce crime in 1990s. The idea with broken windows theory is that small things send potentially big signals about what's tolerated. If a community tolerates small things like broken windows, it invites bigger problems.

To deploy the theory, NYPD started cracking down on a bunch of things they had previously deemed too small to worry about: Turnstile jumpers, subway vandalism, street prostitution, and unsolicited windshield washing. Deliberately broadcasting steady signals about small things seemed to have a big impact. A few years into Bratton's tenure, the felonies (including homicides) were down nearly 50 percent.

While it's easy to look past small things in organizations, broken windows theory applies here, too. Here's an example related by Christy Kenny, director of human resources at PSEG, talking about her experience shifting culture at a nuclear plant:

> We used to do culture training for everyone here. The vendor was good, and it involved some very compelling concepts. But it never got any traction. And that's because the delivery was focused on the fifth frequency—formal communication— while the signals on the other four frequencies were a little out of whack.
>
> The real cultural transformation started when our Chief Nuclear Officer and the rest of the leadership team started reflecting on the disconnects and calling each other out on them. A lot of it has to do with the small signals. Here's an example: On the fifth frequency, we're constantly communicating about safety. One of the standards is that you don't walk and text at the same time.
>
> But people get busy. And the rationalization is, "C'mon. I can walk and chew gum at the same time. I can walk and text at the same time, too." But, no. If employees see a disconnect between what leaders say and what leaders do, it invites them to follow suit. Why would they listen to our safety messages if we can't get our signals straight?
>
> Now we have a culture where we call each other out, even for the little things. That's one of the things that's helped significantly reshape our culture. That's one of the things that contributed to significantly improving plant performance. For example, Hope Creek just completed its first ever breaker-to-breaker run over the last 30-plus years of operation to date. That means the longest stretch of uninterrupted power generation in the plant's history.

The power of Cultura Metro

You know which major city has recently seen a far more impressive drop in crime than the one New York experienced in the nineties?

Fans of the Netflix series Narcos may be surprised to know the answer is Medellin, Colombia, where the crime rate has dropped 90 percent from the end of the Pablo Escobar-era.

Lots of things have contributed to the city's transformation—but one of the most important is the installation of an extensive public transportation system that includes two major subway lines—as well as aerial cable cars and even escalators that carry residents up and down the city's steep mountainsides.

Why has this had such a positive impact? First and foremost, it has made it practical for Paisas (Medellin residents) from even the poorest neighborhoods to get to other parts of the city where there are jobs—as well as educational and cultural opportunities.

But that's not the only reason, according to the locals with whom we spoke during a recent visit. The Metro's leadership realized that with so many Paisas utilizing the system, they had an opportunity to shift the city's culture—on and off the system. So they designed and deliberately perpetuated something Paisas fondly reference as "cultura metro," or Metro Culture. Cultura metro involves a lot of small signals. For example, these things simply are not tolerated on the Metro: pushing or trying to get on the train while others are getting off; food and drinks (not even water!); and graffiti. What is explicitly encouraged: giving up your seat to seniors and being polite. As a result, it's cleaner and more orderly than most public transportations in the U.S.

When you disembark from the Metro, an announcement invites passengers to take cultura metro with them out into the rest of the city. Because so many Paisas do, Medellin has become a vibrant place to live and an inviting place to visit.

Excuse #5: "My high performers will pick up the slack." One of Jeff's brothers, Jeremy, is a professor of musicology, and nearly every summer he spends a few months in Bali working with gamelan musicians. From one of his first trips, he emailed:

> An old man always hangs out at our rehearsals. For some reason, he and I ended up sitting next to each other once, and he started talking to me, and I looked confused, and he cackled and elbowed me in the ribs. This has become our routine. Each day I sit next to him, he talks to me, I grin and shake my head, and he cackles and hits me. Finally, someone translated for me. Apparently, he was saying, "I'm an old man, so I don't have to worry about taking care of kids or working. So I just go to the temple and pray and think about God all day long. What? You don't speak Indonesian? You're so stupid! I'm going to hit you now! Ha!"

A similar routine plays out in many of the organizations where we've worked. Many managers seem to say to their top performers, "I don't have the discipline to replace or hold my poor performers accountable. But *you* keep accepting every new assignment I give you. You're so stupid! I'm going to give you even more work to do now. Ha!" We call it the "Bali Punch." There's a lot of it out there.

In fact, for a majority of the leaders who've completed our Five Frequencies® 360° Profile, "making sure high performers don't get stuck making up for low performers" is one of their three lowest-rated items (of more than 50).

So it's a very common challenge. But loading up high performers instead of doing something about low performers isn't sustainable. It eventually drives away A Players and kills culture.

One of the places where you can encounter the Bali Punch is in the U.S. Department of Defense, where our friend Eric worked. While his coworkers took extra-long coffee breaks, feigning incompetence to avoid assignments, and working on their hobbies (one of his office mates spent his days ordering parts for classic autos), Eric picked up the slack—working extra hours.

When Eric's new boss came on board, he promised there'd be accountability. But he didn't follow through; instead, he made excuses. Eric's boss said, "It's not my fault"; "You need to understand where I'm coming from"; and "You shouldn't question my process." That was apparently why it was necessary for him to give Eric other people's work to do—and then micromanage him.

The problem for Eric was that the Bali Punch worked on him for a long time, and it's because of how he was wired. As the eldest of nine children, he'd learned responsibility early, and he had a strong work ethic. After leaving home, he spent a lot of years in the Army, where the ethos is, "We do more before 8 a.m. than most people do all day." So he is constitutionally incapable of not working hard or slacking like everyone else—even though, strictly speaking, that might be the rational thing to do. But he resented the abuse, and just like Jeremy sitting next to the old man in Bali, Eric eventually walked away.

Excuse #6: "It's always been this way." Here is the last of the common excuses: "This is just the way it is around here." Maintaining the status quo culture is a good idea, if it's already a sustainable source of competitive advantage. But if you want things to be different, you've got to do things differently. Including what's tolerated (or isn't).

That was Nick Akins's philosophy when he became CEO of American Electric Power. "I don't tolerate autocratic, intimidating leadership," he told us. "I lived through some of that. I came up through a culture that was very top-down and very intimidating. A culture where executives had their own dining room. When I became CEO, we did away with that—we sit in the cafeteria just like everybody else."

And he insisted on 360° reviews of all leadership. "Because we have to be able to see how they engage their employees," he said. "If you've got employees going home with their stomach in knots, they are probably not going to be successful. And if you have supervisors who are making them feel that way, we'll develop them or replace them."

Signal Boost #5: Equip people for Moments of Truth

In a famous study conducted some years ago at Princeton Theological Seminary, researchers recruited a group of young seminarians and prepared them to give a talk on the Parable of the Good Samaritan. In this parable, a traveler on the road to Jericho is robbed and beaten by thieves who leave him half-dead. A priest comes along, sees the beaten traveler, and passes by. And then an assistant priest does the same. Finally, a Samaritan arrives on the scene, bandages the man's wounds, brings him to an inn, and takes care of him.

After the researchers prepared the seminarians to give a talk on the story and its implications, they sent the students off, one by one, to fulfill their assignment. Some were directed to move very quickly and told, "You're already late. They were expecting you a few minutes ago." But there was no rush for the others, who were told, "It will be a few minutes before they need you, but you might as well head over."

On the way to their assignment, each seminarian encountered a man on the sidewalk, slumped over, coughing and moaning. Unbeknownst to the seminarians, this man was a confederate—an actor who was part of the experiment.

Of the seminarians instructed to *rush* to their assignment to talk about the Parable of the Good Samaritan, only 10 percent stopped to help the man. The others walked past him—or over him. Meanwhile, a majority of the seminarians in the other group, who weren't in any rush, stopped on their way to speaking about the Good Samaritan to act like one.[11]

What's true of many of the seminarians in this study is also true of many employees in the organizations where we've worked. They know what it means to do the right thing. In fact, like the seminarians, they know it well enough that they can explain it to others, at least in theory. But when they encounter high-pressure "moments of truth" where "doing the right thing" and completing an assigned task (or otherwise "getting results" or pursuing other self-interests) seem to them mutually exclusive options, they often make the wrong choice.

Think about any self-inflicted business crisis of the recent past; for example, the BP oil spill. Like this event, the failure you're thinking of was most likely, rooted in employees making a series of bad choices in Moments of Truth.

Part of the challenge is that most organizations do a lousy job of preparing their employees for these moments. Nassim Taleb doubts it's even possible.[12]

> People whose survival depends on qualitative "job assessments" by someone of higher rank in an organization cannot be trusted for critical decisions. Although employees are reliable by design, it remains the case that they cannot be trusted in making decisions, hard decisions, anything that entails serious tradeoffs. ... The employee has a very simple objective function: fulfill the tasks that his or her supervisor deems necessary, or satisfy some gameable metric.

He's not wrong about the dynamics at play here. But his analysis also points to the solution that we've seen successfully implemented. Managing Moments of Truth™ involves leaders engaging their teams around realistic choices with which they might actually be faced, aligning expectations about the right behavior in those situations, and committing to employees that "when you do the right thing in a Moment of Truth, I (and the rest of the leadership team) will have your back."

Here's one example. A nuclear power plant was preparing for its next refueling outage. A refueling outage is something that plants typically do every 18 months. It involves replacing about one third of the plant's fuel and completing routine maintenance and repairs. It's incredibly complex and expensive, and if it goes well, takes about a month.

The previous outage at this plant had gone terribly. In fact, it had probably been one of the worst in the plant's four decades of operation. Not too far into that outage, a few things went wrong that threw the schedule off. That's an expensive proposition, because keeping the outage going longer not only sucks up more resources and money, it also means the plant isn't generating electricity, and therefore revenue, for the parent company.

As employees felt the pressure to get the outage back on schedule, they took some shortcuts. As a result, a couple of people were hurt (thankfully not permanently) in industrial accidents. They made some sloppy choices that actually further slowed the outage, so that it ultimately went more than three weeks past the original deadline. And, along the way, they hid some mistakes (again, taking shortcuts) that ended up throwing the plant back offline not too long after the outage had finally ended.

Shortly after the unsuccessful outage, the parent company brought in new leadership. The new Chief Nuclear Office set about shifting the culture. We helped him establish a culture metric and get a baseline reading. With strong and steady signals on Five Frequencies®, he and his team began to move the needle. As culture measurably improved, plant performance followed.

Everything was moving in the right direction. But as the next refueling outage approached, there was concern. This would be a real test of whether the culture was truly changing for the better. What would employees do when they encountered Moments of Truth? Take shortcuts? Or do the right thing?

To increase the likelihood of the latter, we helped the CNO run a Moments of Truth exercise to equip every employee (and contractor) for Moments of Truth.

First, we conducted qualitative interviews with department leaders, front-line supervisors, and individual contributors to identify Moments of Truth they'd encountered in past outages. Then we used the data to create customized scenarios for each department. For example:

- A person approaches you. He is one of those people who has a reputation for finding problems with everything. Today, he says he is upset because he reported a problem to his supervisor, but his supervisor hasn't done anything about it. He says that the drywell is about to be closed up. [Engineering]

- You are the only supervisor in the shop. You lead a pre-job brief with a crew that is newly qualified. It's a simple and routine job. You ask if there are any questions and nobody says anything. Hopefully that means they understand. [Maintenance]

- When an issue came up from the field, you decided it would be faster to work it within your discipline. When you are almost at closure, you realize there is one other issue you should have considered that involves another group. [Outage Control Center]

- You get a call from someone escorting two visitors. The paperwork for the first visitor is correct, but you notice a small inconsistency for the second visitor. You tell the escort that she needs to resubmit the form. She says, "Are you sure? This visitor has been here before and I don't have anyone who can fill out the template again for me." [Security]

Next, the CNO called a supervisors-and-above meeting. He said, "As you know, our goal for the upcoming outage is 'a 30-day outage done the right way.' While you're focusing on the first part—30 days—I don't want you to miss the second part: Done the right way."

He explained that done the right way meant that employees follow all the standards, even when it's inconvenient. He emphasized the importance of "stopping when unsure," instead of plowing ahead with an action that could lead to problems. He said he'd rather have an outage done the right way that goes a few days past a deadline, than a 30-day outage done the wrong way (e.g., managed via shortcuts).

He introduced the Moments of Truth concept. He conceded that he hadn't always done the right thing during Moments of Truth. In fact, he acknowledged that only a few months back, he'd realized he was going to be late for a 6 a.m. meeting within the plant's protected area, so he took a shortcut walking through the parking lot (violating a safety standard) to save 43 seconds. He said he recognized almost instantly it was a mistake and he committed to learn from the experience.

Importantly, he acknowledged that during past outages, when employees had tried to do the right thing and live the standards during Moments of Truth, leadership had not always had their backs. Rather, operating outside the standards had been tolerated, even encouraged, if it helped move things along.

He equipped all the leaders in the room with the materials they'd need to lead a conversation with their teams around Moments of Truth, and to realign expectations about how they'd be handled. The conversations cascaded through the plant. Directors met with their teams. Then managers met with their teams. Then supervisors met with individual contributors. There were no PowerPoint presentations—simply structured conversations. At every level, the leaders and employees talked about the Moments of Truth they could face in the upcoming outage. They talked openly about the shortcuts they'd sometimes taken in the past. They talked about what they were committing to do in the upcoming outage. The conversation ended with the leader affirming: "When you do the right thing in a Moment of Truth, I will have your back. The CNO will have your back."

Over a four-week period, every employee participated in a Moments of Truth conversation with their immediate leader and peers.

Employees took it to heart. After the outage started, employees and leaders frequently invoked the concept. Plant leadership used the daily newsletter to recognize instances where employees had done the right thing. (This is Frequency 2, rewarding what you want to see more of). These stories also showed employees that leaders were serious about having their backs.

The result? We'll let the CNO tell you. Here's the note he sent to employees the morning before a site-wide celebration of the outage's completion:

> In the weeks leading up to the outage, I talked a lot about our goals: complete the outage in 30 days, complete all the planned work, do the work error free and, most importantly, keep

everybody safe. I also said that if the outage runs 33 or 34 days, but we hit the marks on safety, scope and error-free work we would be successful. You might remember that I also said if we finished the outage in 28 days, but somebody gets hurt or we have to do a lot of rework to fix errors – that would be a failure.

Well, we were successful!!! You probably know the numbers: 33 days, zero recordable injuries, 99.9 percent of the work complete with just four scope deletions. If you look at this outage against all the previous outages, this was the most successful in plant history.

Before the outage, we introduced the idea of Moments of Truth – which challenged us to make the right decision when faced with a choice. Do you do what's most convenient, or do you choose to do things the right way, even though it may take longer and require more work? I heard Moments of Truth being discussed often when I was out in the plant, so I know we were thinking about our choices and choosing to do the right thing. To me, that's the most important measure of success because that means we are taking care of each other, keeping each other safe and taking good care of the plant.

Enjoy today's celebration. You've earned it.

Chief Nuclear Officers are not the only leaders who want to feel more confident that their employees are equipped for Moments of Truth. We've successfully deployed the approach, for example, in finance, health care, construction, IT, and an airline. Again, the requisite requirements for success are leader-led, no-BS conversations about actual Moments of Truth that employees are likely to encounter, with a commitment that when employees do the right thing, leaders will have their backs.

Signal Boost #6: Be smart about what you *do* tolerate

This chapter has mostly focused on what effective leaders don't tolerate as they shift culture for competitive advantage. But this last Signal Boost acknowledges that it's also important to consider what you *should* tolerate.

For example, more and more, leaders are seeing the advantages of tolerating flexibility. Case in point is the pharma exec who, earlier in her career in academics, was "such a stickler" for people coming in at a particular time and leaving at a particular time. "I always wanted to make sure I was watching my reports and they were doing their work," she told us.

One day an employee approached her. "Look, I can't stay later than four o'clock because I need to pick up my kids," the employee said. "And sometimes in the morning I just can't be here at nine o'clock."

The exec's response: "Well, you know, sorry: You really have to be."

"And that was a mistake," she said, "because my employee quit. She was a really good worker and if I had been flexible, she would have stayed."

"Now, I am very different," this executive says. "I prefer to trust people to do their work instead of having to see them all the time. It makes for a more relaxed atmosphere. *So long as they're doing their job*, I will let them have flexibility. I no longer say anything to somebody about when they're here or where they're working.

"I learned the hard way," she said.

Which brings us to what is probably the most important thing great culture-shifting leaders deliberately tolerate: Making mistakes.

Mistakes are inevitable in any organizational setting. But if they're not tolerated, employees will put their energy into hiding them, minimizing them, and making excuses. (Remember what we said earlier in the chapter: Humans are awesome at this.) When mistakes are tolerated, there's an opportunity to learn from them.

As author Nassim Taleb says in *Skin in the Game*,[13] "making some types of errors is the most rational thing to do, when the errors are of little cost, as they lead to discoveries. For instance, most medical 'discoveries' are accidental to something else. An error-free world would have no penicillin, no chemotherapy... almost no drugs, and most probably no humans."

So mistakes can be the most rational thing. But elsewhere in the same book, Taleb says: "The only definition of rationality that I've found that is practically, empirically, and mathematically rigorous is the following: what is rational is that which allows for survival...Anything that hinders one's survival at an individual, collective, tribal, or general level is, to me, irrational."

You can see the problem: Our success depends on turning errors into opportunities. But what's rational, in many organizational settings, is for employees to hide mistakes instead of learning from them. Sure, *physical* survival is not *literally* jeopardized, not usually. But careers, livelihoods, egos, and other important things are.

Here's an example of a culture where it's irrational to admit (and therefore learn from) excuses—and this one might keep you up at night: If North Korea were ever to launch a ballistic missile at the United States, we'd count on the U.S. Navy's 7th Fleet to counter it. So it was cause for concern in 2017 when two destroyers in the fleet collided at sea, killing 17 sailors. People wondered: "What did that say about the 7th Fleet's effectiveness?" Hopefully, this tragedy inspired leadership to learn from their mistakes and clean up their act. But later in 2017, the *Navy Times*[14] reported that a climate of fear pervaded at least one other ship in the fleet, the Shiloh.

Sailors reported that "minor on-the-job mistakes often led to time in the brig, where they would be fed only bread and water." Applying Taleb's definition, it would be irrational for anyone on that ship, upon making an error or experiencing a near-miss, to draw attention to it and engage others in fixing it and learning from it.

According to sailors quoted in the article, "It's only a matter of time before something horrible happens." Said another: "I just pray we never have to shoot down a missile from North Korea," a distraught sailor lamented, "because then our ineffectiveness will really show."

Yikes! On the flipside, here's an example that'll help calm your nerves, at least if you're a frequent flyer: The air traffic control system is a place where tolerating mistakes is done right. There, they practice what's called "just culture." This is...

> ...an ethos which dictates the way mistakes are reported in the profession, and what the consequences are for human error. The system...involves responding to errors with training and support, not punishment or job loss. More than a buzzword, just culture involves a literal contract that codifies the ways that employees will be made to feel psychologically safe at work,

and it's signed by management and the controller's trade unions.

Importantly just culture doesn't let willful, deliberate (sometimes criminal) actions off the hook. However, we are all human, and humans make mistakes... So if the controller makes an honest mistake and owns up to it, then that's absolutely fine. They will get training... If somebody puts a hand up and says, 'These two aircraft got too close,' for example, that's only positive, there's no blame attached.[15]

The key to "strategic tolerance" is striking a balance. When you decide to become more tolerant of some things (like where people work), you must become, if anything, less tolerant of other things (like the work not getting done). As Harvard professor Gary P. Pisano puts it:[16]

> A tolerance for failure requires an intolerance for incompetence. A willingness to experiment requires rigorous discipline. Psychological safety requires comfort with brutal candor. Collaboration must be balanced with individual accountability.

Fail to manage these tensions and you'll fail to sustain the intended culture shift.

How you show up informally will have big impact on how well you do this. That's the topic of the next chapter.

Mixed signals make people crazy

Sometimes organizations jam their own signals, pitting Frequency 2 against Frequency 3. For example, on the social media site Reddit, user redkinoko described a company in a neighboring building:

> They had an entire area devoted to foosball, pinball, billiards, console gaming, and videoke booths on the ground floor and it was clearly visible because of the glass windows on street level. Oddly enough, nobody ever used them, and the place was almost always empty save for a few people who used the internet kiosks.
>
> When I learned a friend worked there, I asked why nobody would want to take the opportunity to use the awesome-looking recreational facility, he told me that people who do use the facility often found it used against them during performance evaluations, even when their use wasn't excessive at all. After a while word got around and they started avoiding the place altogether. The irony is that their recruitment ads always touts a culture of "work hard, play hard."

Other users chimed in to say that "work hard, play hard" is a red flag when looking at job ads. Said one: "It basically translates to: We are overworked, underpaid, and all semi-functioning alcoholics."

Signal Boost Summary

Want to turn your culture into a source of competitive advantage? Here's a recap of six Signal Boosts on Frequency 3:

- **Remember, you're defined by what you tolerate:** This is true even if you transmit all the right signals on the other four frequencies.

- **Set it and forget it:** Consistency in what's (not) tolerated bolsters culture and streamlines business decision-making.

- **Align your cold signals:** It's important to line up your cold signals with the behavior and performance you don't want to see any more of. Because you will almost always get more of what you tolerate. There are two kinds of cold signals: Those focused on course correction and those focused primarily on punishment (in pursuit of justice and deterrence). If you get good at the former, you'll need less of the latter.

- **Lose your excuses:** You don't want to feel bad. You feel held hostage. It's just a small thing. I can't hold this person accountable. My high performers will pick up the slack. It's always been this way. All are excuses to tolerate stuff you shouldn't. All of them are costly.

- **Equip people for Moments of Truth.** Are your people confident that if they do the right thing, even when it's inconvenient or they're tempted to do something else, that you will have their backs? If they're confident about what's truly expected and what's not tolerated in Moments of Truth, you can feel more confident, too.

- **Be smart about what you do tolerate.** Like work flexibility for people getting results. Or tolerating mistakes when they're accompanied by learning.

CHAPTER 4

FREQUENCY 4: HOW YOU SHOW UP INFORMALLY

FIVE FREQUENCIES

Frequency 4: How you show up informally

This chapter covers three signal boosts for turning culture into competitive advantage

- **Remember: Showing up informally starts with showing up, period**
- **Relinquish your rafts**
- **Change the conversation**

Marketing consultant Gene Marks tells a story[1] about flying out of Buffalo on a regional jet. After take-off, the plane ascended a few thousand feet but stopped climbing. Shortly afterward, the pilot announced over the intercom that something was wrong: The landing gear seemed to be stuck. They'd continue at low altitude while they burned off fuel before returning to the airport and "attempting to land."

Gene happened to be sitting next to a uniformed pilot who was commuting back to his home base in Philadelphia. Before take-off, they'd exchanged greetings, after which the pilot proceeded to pull his cap over his eyes and commence napping.

With malfunctioning landing gear, was the plane in mortal danger? For cues, Gene looked to the pilot sitting next to him. Surely, other passengers did, too. The pilot continued to nap.

Fortunately, and finally, the plane landed safely. Before departing the plane, Gene turned to the pilot and asked if he was aware of what had happened while he was napping. The pilot said he was fully aware and conceded he was "shitting myself" the whole time. But he knew how he "showed up" in this situation would have an impact on all the passengers and he knew there was no value in creating panic. Continuing to nap was the best thing he could do to manage the micro-culture around him.

Like the pilot, you send powerful signals through how you "show up" in informal, unscripted situations. Where you go (or don't), what you say (or don't), how you say it (and to whom), and your non-verbal cues: All these things and more can transmit meaning on Frequency 4. The only question is whether, like the pilot, you're intentional and strategic about it.

§§§§§

As our colleague, Leadership Circle CEO Bill Adams, puts it, "leaders bring the weather."

What does he mean by "weather"?

> It's the way we show up to our people, how we tend to respond to certain situations or crises, what is and is not permissible to discuss, and much more.

> When a great leader walks into the room, everyone is on notice and everyone notices—the energy is palpable. The tone, mood, presence, focus, and behavior of the leader is the weather in any organization—a force of nature. And everyone who works there can feel it, see it, experience it, and describe how it impacts them and those around them. They know if this weather either supports what they are trying to create or destroys it. They can describe if the weather brings out the best in individual employees and teams, or if it lowers their performance. They know if they should relax, contribute, and take risks, or remain cautious, reserved, and careful. Leaders bring the weather, and they define to a large degree what can and can't happen in their organizations.[2]

Whether you call it "bringing the weather" or "strong, steady signals on Frequency 4," it's easy to see how the way you show up informally can have a huge impact on your organization's culture: It can make it a source of competitive advantage...or the exact opposite.

As we said in the book's introduction, part of our job is helping senior leaders measurably define their desired-state culture, the culture that makes sustainable business success both *possible* and *probable*. Many of our clients can't achieve or maintain competitive advantage without more speed, agility, and innovation. So when we're helping them define their desired-state culture, they often conclude they need employees to more consistently *feel* empowered to speak up, solve problems, suggest improvements, take smart risks and make positive changes. They also need employees to more consistently take initiative and "fail fast," learning from experiments and mistakes instead of minimizing or rationalizing them.

Employees won't feel or do these things for long unless they perceive they operate in a culture that provides psychological safety. Your signals across all Five Frequencies determine whether that psychological safety is in place. But our predictive analyses show that *signals on Frequency 4—how you show up informally—produce a disproportionate influence.*

But what is psychological safety? Harvard Business School Professor Amy Edmondson[3] coined the term 20 years ago. Here's how she defines it:

> In a workplace, psychological safety is the belief that the environment is safe for interpersonal risk taking. People feel able to speak up when needed — with relevant ideas, questions, or concerns — without being shut down in a gratuitous way. Psychological safety is present when colleagues trust and respect each other and feel able, even obligated, to be candid.

However:

> …working in a psychologically safe environment does not mean that people always agree with one another for the sake of being nice. It also does not mean that people offer unequivocal praise or unconditional support for everything you have to say. Psychological safety is not an "anything goes" environment where people are not expected to adhere to high standards or meet deadlines. It is not about becoming

"comfortable" at work. Psychological safety enables candor and openness and, therefore, thrives in an environment of mutual respect.

And that's why...

If leaders want to unleash individual and collective talent, they must foster a psychologically safe climate where employees feel free to contribute ideas, share information, and report mistakes.

How important is psychological safety? Google[4] conducted a two-year study of more than 180 of its teams to identify the attributes that determine whether a group turns into one of the company's most or least successful. They expected the results would reveal *who* to put on a team (e.g., "take one Rhodes Scholar, two extroverts, one engineer who rocks at AngularJS, and a PhD"). Instead, Google researchers found that what mattered most—the lever at the top of the list—is whether the members of the team felt they could take risks—and fail—without feeling insecure or embarrassed and without fear of punishment. That is to say: Psychological safety.

In the absence of psychological safety, you are not getting full access to the intellectual horsepower of the A Players you've worked so hard to recruit. As Stanford's Laura Delizonna explains:[5]

The brain processes a provocation by a boss, competitive coworker, or dismissive subordinate as a life-or-death threat. The amygdala, the alarm bell in the brain, ignites the fight-or-flight response, hijacking higher brain centers. This "act first, think later" brain structure shuts down perspective and analytical reasoning. Quite literally, just when we need it most, we lose our minds.

That's true for Rhodes scholars. Engineers who rock at AngularJS. Everybody.

In the rest of this chapter, we'll describe three signal boosts on Frequency 4 that support a psychologically safe work environment. They are distinct but highly inter-related. One of them is about your mere presence. One of them is about your mindset or the leadership "operating system" that governs how you show up. The third one is about how you shape informal conversations.

Signal Boost #1: Remember: Showing up informally starts with showing up, period

An HSBC employee in Taiwan, Jennifer, decided to wed her longtime girlfriend. Jennifer's traditional parents rejected the idea and said they wouldn't attend her wedding. So John Li, Jennifer's boss and the CEO of HSBC Taiwan, walked Jennifer down the aisle instead.[6] Talk about a leader showing up!

Showing up is usually not that dramatic. But being present, listening, responding, showing you care: These acts show that you are a member of your employees' tribe and worthy of their trust. Here are some examples of what that looks like and the cultural and business value it creates.

Go where your people go

"I don't think you can have an accurate understanding of the culture if you're not out there frequently. You can be misled." That's according to Tim Rausch, Chief Nuclear Officer for the Tennessee Valley Authority. So, he blocks off time for "getting out there" three days a week. He often grabs a next-level leader and they walk together. Tim will say to them: "Tell me what you see. Tell me what you hear." He'll watch how that leader interacts with people out in the field. And if he thinks they can be more observant, or more engaging, he'll (discreetly) coach them on the spot.

When he was a plant manager and then a Site VP, he came in on Thanksgiving and Christmas to ask his people how they were doing. They'd typically ask: "Why are you here?" And Tim would say, "Because you are."

On one occasion, the company sent a civil engineer to the top of a 500-foot cooling tower to do a walkdown. Tim asked the engineer: "What are you looking for while you're up there?" The engineer mentioned concrete that's falling or cracking, the handrail weakening, things like that, and then joked: "You should come with me."

Joke or not, Tim thought seriously about it. Tim's boss discouraged it. But Tim said, "If it's not safe for me up there then why are we sending an employee?"

Word of Tim's plans got out and a multitude assembled below to watch him climb the tower, after which he conducted a three-hour inspection with the civil engineer. Tim used the time to ask him if he thought there were ways the plant could better utilize his skillset. Back on the ground, Tim acted on the answers.

That's the kind of leading you can't do from your office.

"Getting out there" is also a good way to equip yourself with an early warning system. In chapter 2, we introduced you to Beth M. Foley, Chief Communications Officer at Edison International. Early in her career, she frequently closed the door to her office, put her head down, and powered through piles of work. "At that time," she recalls, "it seemed logical to me. Our team had a lot of deliverables and I pride myself on meeting commitments."

But later on she realized that getting the work done is only half of the game, if that. "The most important job happens outside of my office," she says. "In today's world, an ember becomes an inferno in a nanosecond, so the benefit of casual conversation with team members, peers and customers is the ability to spot and address small problems as well as identify potential opportunities. You'll rarely unearth nuggets sitting in your office."

Know their names

> Napoleon said men will die for bits of ribbon pinned to their chests, but the General understands that even more men will die for a man who remembered their names, as he does theirs. When he inspects them, he walks among them, eats with them, calls them by their names and asks about wives, children, girlfriends, hometowns. All anyone ever wants is to be recognized and remembered. Neither is possible without the other.

That's from fiction; specifically, Viet Thanh Nguyen's Pulitzer Prize-winning novel, *The Sympathizer*.

But our friend Brad Mills, who we introduced in the last chapter, experienced this phenomenon in real-life as a U.S. Marine. One of Brad's commanders, Andrew Beeler, made a lasting impression. Colonel Beeler seemed to know the names of all 900 people in his battalion.

"The first time he inspected my company," Brad recalls, "he called my Marines by name—and they didn't have name tags. It was astonishing. He also knew if they were married and if they had children. Being in the military is very hard on families. So, when you can call home to your spouse and say, 'The colonel asked about you,' it can make a big difference."

And it had an impact on how Brad showed up, too: "He was the guy who wrote my fitness report, so I felt confident that when he wrote it that he'd have some idea what was going on. That made me feel good." And when Brad became company commander, he emulated his role model. "I invested time studying the roster so I could call people by name."

But it's about more than just knowing names. "We used to say, your job is to accomplish the mission and look after your Marines. If there's a hair's breadth of difference between the two, mission takes priority," Brad says. But the welfare of the Marines is right below that. He remembers a complicated training run in the middle of a cold night. "We came back to the rallying point at 2 a.m. and there was the colonel serving hot coffee. This was a long time ago, so you can tell it left a very memorable impression."

When, like the colonel, you make an investment of time and effort, your people will want to pay it back (in discretionary energy) and, like Brad, pay it forward (making the same kind of effort for those that *they* lead).

Invest in high-quality face time

We often stay at an MGM property because it's located directly across the street from one of our clients. The whole place is well designed and spotless—but even more impeccable is the service. It's the kind of place where you get out of your Uber and the bellman warmly greets you by name, even if your last visit was four months ago.

One evening we were eating at one of the property's four restaurants when a manager dropped by to chat. The restaurant was bustling but this wasn't a perfunctory "how's your meal" drive-by; he asked us questions about our stay, our meals, and our work, and he listened attentively to the answers. It was a thoroughly pleasant conversation. We also learned that his name was Steve Zanella, and he wasn't just the restaurant manager (our original assumption), but the general manager of the entire hotel and casino property.

A few weeks later, we saw him again. He recognized us and we again resumed a warm conversation. "Steve, remember, we're not gamblers," we joked, "we're just here on business. We'll talk forever but you should probably spend your time with your high rollers." He laughed but we kept talking for another ten minutes.

We visited again a few weeks later and learned on that visit that he shared an interest in our favorite topic: turning culture into competitive advantage. Steve told us his leadership agenda was all about driving performance against a very high set of service standards. For that to work in a *sustainable fashion*, he needed to create a culture where employees felt confident they could ask questions and provide feedback. And that required leaders to get out of their offices and spend time on the work floor with employees.

"Is it working?" we asked. "I think so," he said. "I just had a conversation with an employee who stopped me and said, 'Steve, management wants to do x, y, and z. But it doesn't make sense to us.' I said, '*Management?* Who do you think *I* am?' The employee said, 'Sorry about that. I guess I didn't think of you as management.' So, I explained the changes, answered his questions, and he thanked me for connecting the dots so that it all made sense."

A couple of years after we first met Steve, the strong performance of his hotel and casino earned him a promotion. He is now president of CityCenter, one of MGM's premiere properties in Las Vegas.

And now it's been a few years since he last dropped by our dinner table. But we haven't forgotten his three leadership principles for shaping culture by the way you informally "show up."

1. **Be truly present.** "I used to have a boss who would invite me in for one-on-ones but then he'd proceed to read his emails during the conversation," Steve recalls. "What I thought (but never had the courage to say) is: 'Why don't I just go back to my desk and write you an email?' Everyone's time is valuable. If

you aren't committed to being fully engaged in the conversation you're in, you should give that person and yourself back the time."

2. **Take the shoeshine guy to lunch.** "Everyone—both customers and employees—talks to him," Steve said. "He can tell you what's moving in the right direction—and where we're getting loose and need to tighten up operations. I'd need to conduct a dozen customer and employee focus groups to fill in the gaps if I wasn't having regular check-ins with the shoeshine guy." (If you're not running a hotel or an airport, you probably don't employ a shoeshine guy. But you can likely find the equivalent.)

3. **Use employee events to "live the brand" in a positive way.** "Caring is really at the heart of our brand. And as I was thinking about some interesting ways of engaging employees and breaking down siloes, my wife suggested a pet adopt-a-thon. We partnered with the Humane Society and they brought in 40 animals. We invited all our employees. I was nervous it wouldn't go well. The event started at noon and I decided I'd drop in at 12:20. As soon as I showed up, someone yelled, 'Steve, the animals are all gone!' I said, 'What! They escaped?' 'No, they've all been adopted in 20 minutes.' I should have predicted. When you work hard to promote a culture of caring, and then you give employees a unique opportunity to put that culture into practice, they're going to jump all over it!"

Set the 2 a.m. tone

Pete Sena is President of PSEG Nuclear. A year before he showed up, union leadership had gone off and generated a list of 20 things they were concerned about. This was not the stereotypical list of things like "we're not getting enough overtime" or "there are too many contractors." This was about performance.

They had presented the list to Pete's predecessor and nothing had come of it, apparently. So when they told Pete about the list in their first meeting, he told the union: "I'd like to see the list." They said, "We'll send it tonight." That night Pete received the list and was impressed. At 2 a.m. he wrote them back with a response to each of the specific issues identified.

In some cases, he promised action and thanked them where they'd flagged issues he hadn't yet learned about. In other cases, he shared a different perspective. But he responded to every concern. The 2 a.m. response set the tone for the relationship and his leadership style of proactively addressing problems that has dramatically improved his organization's performance. Everyone is working on the same team.

Of course, it doesn't necessarily require emailing in the middle of the night to produce this outcome. The important thing is that you show up in a way that says: If you've got input on how to improve performance, understanding that input will always be a high priority for me.

Show up and suffer together

Jose-Luis Bretones-Lopez, founder and managing partner of Linar Advisors, once worked as executive vice president of a global, publicly traded metals distribution company, overseeing a vast (and troubled) supply chain operation. "When I came in, one of the problems was that nobody knew how much inventory we had," he says. So he made the dramatic decision to stop the normal flow of materials in and out of the company for a long weekend in order to conduct a physical inventory.

Unfortunately, it was August, and three of the company's warehouses were in Houston. It promised to be no fun. "Even though I didn't know the difference between a fracking pipe and a drilling bar, I knew I had to go there and help with the count," Jose-Luis said. In fact, he took his whole team. Working alongside the Houston-based Sales and Ops teams, they put in 16-hour days. And it was as bad, or worse, than anticipated. "Spiders, snakes, humidity…the trifecta of misery."

But Jose-Luis understood the trade-off. If he didn't visibly show up for this painful but critical undertaking, he wouldn't have any credibility the next time he called down to Houston asking for something. After the physical inventory was finished, the newfound credibility was palpable. "And after suffering together," he says, "my team became a better team."

Another collateral benefit: Houston's Sales and Ops teams had a history of pointing fingers at one another. But after suffering together for three days, they learned they liked each other more than they expected. And as a merged tribe, they became in the weeks and months that followed exemplars of effective collaboration for the rest of the company.

In summary: As humans, we're hardwired to monitor who is in-tribe and who isn't. That instinct helped our primitive ancestors survive. We'll trust and work harder for those with whom we share our camp. When you show up and suffer together, it sends the subtle signal that you're all in the same tribe.

Signal Boost #2: Relinquish your raft

A traveler on an important journey comes to a raging river. It seems there's no way to cross. And that's terrible news, because this is an important journey. Fortunately, she spots a rickety old raft on the bank, off in the brush. With trepidation, she pushes the raft into the water, hops on, and amazingly, uses it to reach the other side. She's able to continue her important journey. She thinks: I may encounter other raging rivers down the path, so I must keep this raft. So she carries the raft on her back as she continues her journey. It's a heavy raft and it slows her down. When fellow travelers point this out, she's incredulous: "You don't understand," she says. "If it wasn't for this raft, I wouldn't be where I am today!" And she's right. That's literally true. The problem is: If she doesn't put down the raft, she may not get to where she needs to go on her important journey.

Like the traveler in this parable,[†] lots of leaders carry their metaphorical rafts much longer than necessary or useful. For many, the raft takes the form of well-developed and proven Reactive Tendencies. As the name suggests, Reactive Tendencies are operating beliefs and behaviors that help you react to whatever comes your way on any given day, thereby "proving yourself" to your boss or other stakeholders, and then surviving with enough ego strength still intact that you can show up and do the same damn thing tomorrow.

Bill Adams, whom you met earlier in the chapter, has mentored us for more than two decades. And along with Leadership Circle Chairman Bob Anderson, Bill wrote the book (actually, two books[‡]) on reactive leadership systems and the alternative (which we'll get to shortly). Over 20,000 leaders globally utilize the Leadership Circle Profile each year. Altogether, Bill and Bob have gathered data on this topic from over 1 million leaders!

According to Bill, one of the Reactive Tendencies that's helped many leaders make it this far is *Compliance*: learning to be cautious and "going with the flow." It's proven to be just what some have needed at various raging rivers along the way to get validation, avoid rejection, and not have important people get mad at them. Rather than "speak their truth," these leaders heavily caveat what they say and express disagreement through passive aggression. Paul Byrne, another Leadership Circle colleague, sees High Compliance manifest most frequently in business conversations where people are so eager "to get

---

[†] We've heard it from multiple sources, but first from *Buddhism: Plain and Simple* by Steve Hagen.

[‡] *Mastering Leadership* and *Scaling Leadership*, both published by Wiley.

on the same page" that the rush for alignment strips away some of the best ideas before they ever get a hearing.

Another raft that leaders carry is *Protecting*. This Reactive Tendency can take the form of being smartly cynical and emotionally distant or arrogantly aloof. If you've got a heavy reliance on Protective Tendencies—and if you're forced to choose—you'd rather be "right" than "effective," since being right is part of the "leader brand" you've carefully curated. As Paul says, "Many of these leaders devote their best energy each day to what they perceive as their number one job task: Watching their own back. Solving business problems gets the brain capacity that's leftover." Others advance their journey to a certain point by learning to roll their eyes and be snarky as a means of shielding their ego from what they view as a raging river of BS that could otherwise overwhelm them. Needless to say, when High-Protecting leaders fail to play full out, business value is inevitably lost.

The third big Reactive Tendency is *Controlling*. And it might be the most common. Many leaders have made it this far on their journey by exerting control. They literally wouldn't be where they are today if their perfectionism, overbearing nature, micromanagement, and autocratic tendencies hadn't helped them navigate a raging river or two. The core operating belief, Bill says, is "I'm okay if I am the one who gets results, am perfect, am moving up, am in charge and in control." But since these leaders "often seek and gain power at the expense of others— seeing others as resources to be used to achieve what they want—they do not delegate, develop teamwork, build trust, or mentor others gracefully."

Because each day involves the ego-driven pursuit of perfection, High Controllers tend to discount or ignore negative feedback and "believe their own press." This makes them vulnerable, though they'd deny it. Another challenge? "When you go high on controlling, it takes a toll on relationships," Paul says. "And in complex, decentralized organizations—where influence has become more important than control as a means of getting things done—you need relationships to lead effectively."

Whether it's Complying, Protecting, or Controlling, a Reactive Tendency becomes like the traveler's raft, hobbling important leadership journeys. "Make no mistake about it," Bill says. "Reactive leaders can and do get results, and these results are sometimes extraordinary. They may sell more, innovate more, and deliver more than anyone else in the organization. However, High-Reactive leaders often achieve extraordinary results at the expense of those who report to and work with them. The people around them feel at risk, vulnerable, unsafe. Not a good environment for smart risk taking, agility, and innovation. Over time, you get rapidly diminishing returns."

In short, the results achieved by carrying the treasured raft aren't sustainable. "A primarily Reactive leadership style severely limits scale," Bill says. To invoke a phrase that we introduced in chapter 1, High-Reactive leaders are short-term rather than long-term greedy.

But in one important way, Reactive leaders are different than the traveler in the parable. The traveler in the parable knew she was carrying a raft! For most High-Reactive leaders, the Reactive

Tendencies they keep doubling down on are not even something they're conscious of. They've been codified into the operating systems in their heads that govern their leadership behavior.

As Bill says, "The structure of our operating system focuses our attention, influences our choices, drives our behavior, and determines the effectiveness of our actions (both short- and long-term). Therefore, consciousness is the operating system of performance. We cannot perform at a higher level of performance than is built into our operating system."

To upgrade your OS, you've got to know that it exists and know there's an alternative.

The next-gen OS, Bill and Paul say, is "Creative Mindset." To explain it, let's contrast it with Reactivity.

- When you strip away the veneer, Reactivity is always, ultimately about proving yourself to others as a means of ego "survival." In contrast, Creative Mindset is more internally driven by what you care about and ultimately want to stand for.

- In many ways, Reactivity is about playing not to lose. So does Creative Mindset mean playing to win? "Yes, but more accurately 'playing for purpose,'" Bill says. It's about keeping your eye on the prize. It's about focusing energy on creating long-term outcomes that you find truly meaningful.

- Creative leaders speak their truth and are courageously authentic. They're willing to talk about difficult-to-talk-about topics and manage conflict and disagreements in support of important long-term outcomes.

- Just like High-Reactive leaders, High-Creative leaders have good days and bad days. On the good days, High-Creatives build momentum toward their vision. After the bad days, they pick themselves up and dust themselves off, get refocused, learn from their mistakes, recalibrate their plans, and continue on the journey—re-centered rather than depleted.

- With a Creative Mindset, leaders are less impulsive and more curious and reflective than their Reactive counterparts. Forced to choose, they'd rather be effective than "right." They are more agile managing uncertainty; they don't pretend they know how everything is going to go, but they do know which direction they want to face, how they want to show up in the world, and how they want to influence what emerges.

- Creative leaders tend to love people and feel comfortable partnering with others. They believe that helping to bring out the best in others is core to what it means to lead. They're confident they can find ways to expand the pie versus carving it up in a way that reserves for themselves the biggest slice. (People are clearly important to Creative leaders, but at the same time, they're not looking to others for constant validation.)

Why does this all this matter? According to Bill and Paul and FCG's enormous database, a majority of leaders—all across the globe—continue to rely on primarily Reactive Operating Systems. Obviously, this has an impact on how these leaders show up informally. According to the dataset, High-Creative leaders are dramatically more likely than Reactive leaders to demonstrate strong people skills (caring, compassionate, big-hearted, respectful)—and to be good listeners and team builders.

But is all of this just feel-good, corporatized Buddhism or is Creative Mindset a genuine source of competitive advantage? Again, the data make a strong case. Bill's research team found a .93 correlation between ratings of leaders' Creative Competencies and ratings of their leadership effectiveness (measured as an independent variable). In other words, the more you demonstrate Creative Mindset, the more effective the people around you consider you to be. Conversely, the team found a negative (-.68) correlation between leadership effectiveness and Reactive Tendencies. The more you continue to double down on what brought you this far, the less effective you are rated to be.

But what about actual business performance? That's where the proverbial rubber meets the road. The research team found a .61 correlation between ratings of leadership effectiveness and business performance (measured in terms of market share, profitability, return on assets, and quality). That makes for a strong business case: Shifting to a Creative Mindset is good for leaders, good for the people they lead, good for culture, and good for business.§

Avoid the pull of personal heroics

Here's a story about Reactive Tendencies and the ego-gratifying stories we tell ourselves about their indispensability.

---

§ Read Bill Adams and Bob Anderson's *Scaling Leadership* for a much deeper dive into the data. Despite its basis in heavy-duty research, the book is very clear, accessible, and practical.

Back in the day, Jeff and his brother Greg used to ride their road bikes together at least 50 miles per week. But one day, Greg called to express concern that Jeff hadn't been on his bike for two months. Jeff had been working on a huge project and hadn't exercised in weeks. He looked down from his laptop at his belly creeping farther and farther over his belt and concluded Greg was right. So he agreed that he should take a break for a Saturday afternoon ride of 20 miles.

Greg was a couple of weeks away from a 200-mile endurance ride for which he'd been training for months. So he'd already put in 50+ miles earlier in the day before Jeff joined him. The two brothers set off on one of their regular routes, which included a steep hill, rising nearly 1,000 feet in less than a mile. Halfway through the climb, Jeff completely lost his breath. Meanwhile, Greg was talking and breathing regularly, maintaining an efficient, sustainable pace.

Suddenly, an enormous, snarling black dog raced toward the cyclists from a nearby porch. Though moments before Jeff had nearly reached his physical limits, the threat of a vicious canine coming after him provoked an adrenaline spike, and he found the energy to pump a little faster up the hill. Just fast enough that Jeff reached the boundaries of the dog's imagined territory before the dog did. The dog retreated to his porch where his embarrassed owner quickly hauled him inside.

Catching his breath, Jeff looked back and realized Greg was standing in the road, straddling his bike, not far from the spot he'd been when the dog first charged toward them. "Dude, what are you doing?" Jeff asked.

"Dude, what are *you* doing?" Greg replied. "You were about to drop over dead, Cujo comes after you, and you try to outrun him *uphill?*"

"Yeah, I guess that made no sense," Jeff conceded. "What did you do?"

"Well, first, I figured that since you're slow and out of shape, he was going to chase *you*. And that proved correct. But I pulled out my water bottle to throw at him or squirt him, if necessary. And I figured if I had to outrun him, I'd significantly improve my odds by turning around and riding *downhill.*"

Both the brothers had PowerTaps on their bikes that display performance metrics, including wattage output. "Wow, I maxed out at about 900 watts coming up the hill," Jeff observed after Greg joined him. Jeff could sustain 900 watts for all of about two seconds. Greg looked down at his readout. "I maxed out at 200 watts on the hill," he said. This was a level of output that a few weeks later Greg would sustain for 18 hours and 200 miles. And yet—though it was perverse and delusional—Jeff was the only brother who concluded the day's ride telling himself that he'd done something truly heroic.

We've seen a similar dynamic play out at least a few times in organizational settings. Clients conclude—at least intellectually—that they want to have a culture that is more outcome-creating and less reactive. They're tired of constant drama and fire drills, they claim. They want to stabilize, establish effective and efficient processes, and become—most of all—**less dependent on personal heroics to produce business results**. With the client, we agree on what it will take to make that happen. They invest in the process. And then they find ways to sabotage those efforts (while maintaining plausible deniability that this is exactly what they're doing).

It turns out they've developed quite the predilection for fleeing Cujo uphill. It makes no business sense. The resulting culture doesn't attract or retain A Players. It's not sustainable. But—Lord have mercy—the adrenaline rush is addictive. It's perverse and delusional. But they go home telling themselves they're doing something heroic.

To return to the language of Signal Boost #2, this is a good "raft to relinquish."

Signal Boost #3: Change the conversation

As our friend Gregg Baron observes, "Everything that happens in an organization happens in or because of a conversation." The implication: If you want to change the culture, you've got to change the conversation. In the rest of this chapter, we'll suggest ways you can "change the conversation" for a particular purpose: Fostering an environment where fear and egos don't get in the way of sharing information, confronting problems, learning from mistakes, and producing important outcomes. We call this Zen Information Flow.

Here's an example of someone taking a risk to promote Zen Information Flow, a decision that proved to have big positive long-term consequences. Two decades ago, Susanna Foo was one of Philadelphia's first celebrity chefs. We had an opportunity to ask her a few years back how she got into the business.

Susanna was born in China and grew up in Taiwan, where her father was a military man—a lieutenant general—and he instilled military discipline at home. Later, she moved to the United States, earned a degree in library science, and married. Susanna's husband's family opened a restaurant. Early on, the restaurant received a very bad review from the local paper, and her husband's family was perplexed and angry. "Why would they do that to us?"

Susanna listened to the grumbling and excuse-making before she spoke up: "I know why," Susanna offered. "The food is not good." With unadorned truth telling, Susanna changed the conversation from victimhood-perpetuation to fact-based problem-solving. And then she jumped into the business and changed everything about the restaurant. And that became the unlikely origin of her culinary stardom.

Unfortunately, when it comes to candor, there aren't enough Susanna Foos to go around. As *Crucial Conversations* co-author Joseph Grenny observes:

> Three decades of researching human behavior has taught me that you can generally measure the health of a team, relationship, or even an entire organization by measuring the average lag time between identifying problems and discussing them. The longer issues go unaddressed, the higher the price you pay in trust, engagement, decision making, productivity, quality, safety, diversity—you name it.
>
> And yet my company's research shows that, in typical organizations, 72 percent of people fail to speak up … People bite their tongue for weeks, months, and sometimes forever. Meanwhile, bad decisions get made, customers are hurt, bad behavior goes unchecked, and employee cynicism festers.[7]

Why is it so hard to candidly confront problems in a way that is open, honest, and direct? As we've said previously, the root problem here is human nature. We—all of us humans—are super defensive. As a species, we wouldn't have survived otherwise. The challenge is our brains are wired to process threats to our egos much the same way they process physical threats. One study found that "hurt feelings activated the same regions of the brain activated by broken bones or other physical injuries."[8] In other words, an ego wounded by critical feedback may, in some ways literally, be in pain. That's why it's hard to handle the truth. We don't want to get hurt. And we (usually) don't want to hurt others.

This is where you and the way you show up in conversations can make a significant difference.

Practice Zen Information Flow: Who can talk to whom

As author Nassim Taleb says, "the classical art of conversation is to avoid any imbalance…people need to be equal, at least for the purpose of the conversation, otherwise it fails. It has to be hierarchy-free and equal in contribution. …Indeed, one can generalize and define a community as a space within which many rules of competition and hierarchy are lifted, where the collective prevails over one's interest."[9]

Here's how Elon Musk, in an all-employee email, communicated this principle in support of Tesla's collective interests:[10]

> There are two schools of thought about how information should flow within companies. By far the most common way is chain of command, which means that you always flow communication through your manager. The problem with this

approach is that, while it serves to enhance the power of the manager, it fails to serve the company.

…Any manager who allows this to happen, let alone encourages it, will soon find themselves working at another company. No kidding.

Anyone at Tesla can and should email/talk to anyone else according to what they think is the fastest way to solve a problem for the benefit of the whole company. You can talk to your manager's manager without his permission, you can talk directly to a VP in another dept, you can talk to me, you can talk to anyone without anyone else's permission. Moreover, you should consider yourself obligated to do so until the right thing happens."

Musk recognizes that he can't compete with the big automakers on size—but the Zen Information Flow he's describing helps Tesla compete on speed, intelligence, and agility.

John Legere, the CEO of T-Mobile, has also established an information flow that's become a source of competitive advantage. He regularly visits retail stores and call centers where, in addition to taking selfies with employees, he engages employees in real, two-way conversation about how to strengthen the customer experience.[11]

"When I go to retail stores," Legere says, "I jokingly tell the employees that everybody between me and them is the enemy. In effect, what I mean is that … if I can hear them and they can hear me, everything will be fine. All we need to do is make sure the entire company understands that it's their job to pass information between us. And so far, so good."

Is it working? Under Legere's leadership, T-Mobile has doubled its customer base.

Practice Zen Information Flow: What's said and how

Research suggests that humans are about five times more sensitive to negative information than to positive information. (Generally, the former creates greater emotional arousal than the latter.) Recognizing this, you can try to shape an organizational discourse that achieves the optimal balance. In other words, make sure that positive information (e.g., good news) outweighs negative information by a 5:1 ratio. A worthwhile endeavor? It's hard to argue with the data. For example, researchers have found that in the most stable marriages, "[T]here is five times as much positive feeling and interaction between husband and wife as there is negative."[12] More relevant to our discussion, a study of work teams and their performance found that the highest-performing teams "averaged 5.6 positive interactions for every negative one," whereas the 19 lowest-performing teams "racked up a positive-negative ratio of 1:3."[13]

That's why we frequently encourage our clients (all of them are leaders) to informally monitor the discourse among their teams over a typical week, estimate the ratio between positive and negative sentiment, and decide whether it should be shifted. One way to shift the ratio is to put more effort into accentuating the positive. Most leaders find there are many more opportunities to do this than they initially realize; it just requires some attention. But you don't want to engage in contrivance, as in "I have two problems that I want us to confront, so I must fabricate 10 pieces of good news to balance it out." That kind of inauthenticity will quickly undermine the psychological safety you're working to create.

And you don't want to shift the ratio by ignoring bad news. That's a guaranteed recipe for trouble. But what if you could achieve and sustain a strong positive:negative ratio by creating a discourse where the negative stuff you have to deal with inside the organization isn't actually experienced *negatively*?

According to neuroscientists Sandra Aamodt and Sam Wang, this is possible, via something called "reappraisal." As they explain, "That's when you reconsider the meaning of an event as a way of changing your feelings about it."[14] As such, it involves disciplining the brain's executive function to override the reptilian inclination to freak out and get defensive. Through reappraisal, the executive function does this by reframing the situation.

Here's an example to illustrate how reappraisal works: It's startling for many Americans the first time they experience the "crazy" traffic in an Asian metropolis, such as Ho Chi Minh City. It flows like water, filling all space available. At any point, your taxi may be one of seven vehicles spread across two lanes. Through frequent stops and starts, you're surrounded by other vehicles (scooters, buses, bikes) three inches ahead of you, behind you, and on both sides. And regardless of whether there is a signal or what it displays, your driver will enter intersections without looking for oncoming traffic. Additionally, because traffic moving in your direction is inevitably slow, your driver will take advantage of any open space in the left lane—even if there's a dump truck coming toward you a block away—then slide back into the right lane just in time to avoid a head-on collision.

And yet you'll probably arrive at your destination without incident. Sure, you'll pass the occasional fender-bender, but they don't seem to occur with more frequency there than anywhere else, especially given the traffic volume. What makes this all possible is the horn—and more specifically, honking. Vietnamese drivers honk constantly. If Americans used horns as much as the Vietnamese do, we'd have road rage and bloodshed every rush hour. Why? Because we honk our horns and perceive others' honking their horns primarily as an expression of ego and an assertion of relative social power. (Here in Philadelphia, where we live, horn honking is typically accompanied by a hand gesture featuring the middle finger.) In Vietnam, though, horn honking is a purely task-focused or functional activity. It just means "I'm *here*." Not "*I'm* here, you stupid piece of $###!"

So, after you've spent a few days there on the roads, you naturally reappraise what it means to hear someone honking; in this new context, honking goes from something negative to something constructive that promotes mobility and safety. How cool would it be if people on your team reappraised what it meant to confront mistakes, or to try something and fail, or to hear a suggestion for how to think or do things differently? What if it all landed as non-threatening information—so that the subsequent mental processing occurs up front in the executive brain rather than back in the reptilian bits?

In the rest of this chapter, we'll explore some ways to do this by changing the conversation, promoting Zen Information Flow through what you say and how you say it.

Contract for candor. When someone shares critical feedback, and it catches us by surprise or we perceive that in delivering the information they have violated a (probably unwritten) social contract, we're likely to feel personally attacked.

Explicitly contracting for candor can change that.

Contracting for candor means negotiating explicit jurisdiction with others about how you're committed to communicating. That way, when you disagree or exchange critical feedback, you're less likely to be triggered by an unpleasant surprise. When your reptile brain starts to detect a personal attack, your executive function can step in and say, "Wait a second. This is just something predictable that we agreed to do."

Here's a "contracting for candor" example from our friend Dale Vines, who leads teams in industrial plants:

> There's a conversation I like to have every time I get a new employee—or a new boss. I say something like this: "You and I may not agree. All I ask is that we listen to one another. Let's lay out why we disagree. Both of us. And at the end of the day if there's still disagreement the person with the highest position generally gets to make that decision. That's part of life. But the important thing is that we understand the whys and the concerns and we each feel like we have been heard.

Dale adds:

> In both the boss and the subordinate role, there are times when I have listened to somebody and realized I was about to make a very stupid mistake because I did not fully understand potential impacts or alternatives. And sometimes I learn something new but still conclude my original position was the right one. But having that open, honest, and direct conversation changes the dynamic. That's why I love having people who feel comfortable enough to disagree with me; not for argument's sake, but to ensure we arrive at higher quality decisions.

We worked with a supply chain executive a few years back who contracted for candor with his new chief of staff. He had taken on an enormous challenge. He knew that to be successful, he'd need access to unfiltered information. "I committed to deliver hundreds of millions of dollars in cost savings in a relatively short period of time. You can't take on an aggressive goal like that —and succeed at it—if you're mired in wishful thinking," he told us. "Reliable information about what's working and what isn't—even if it's unpleasant—makes it possible to recalibrate as we go, to ensure the right outcome."

Early in his career, he'd encountered a leader who'd asked his staff to complete a 360-degree evaluation. When the leader didn't like the not-as-positive-as-hoped-for results, he sent it back to the team to redo it. It made an impression. "I vowed I would never be the kind of leader who claims to want to know the truth but really doesn't have the appetite for it."

When he informed us that he was looking for a chief of staff, we told him about a qualified candidate in another department. We'd worked with her in the past—but we warned him that she had once described him to us, based on a single, fleeting encounter, as "an unmitigated jackass." To his mind, that didn't disqualify her from consideration; in fact, just the opposite: He immediately sought her out and hired her. They explicitly agreed that part of her role was to tell him what he needed to know but most likely didn't.

Another way to contract for candor is to make feedback exchange a non-elective activity, something built into standard operating procedures. For example, if your organization is like most, you conduct lessons learned sessions (to discuss what worked and what didn't) only after projects that go badly. But when the calendaring of a lessons learned session signals something bad, the participants (especially the ones who most need to learn from their mistakes) will show up with a defensive attitude. However, if "lessons learned" is something that you always do, even when a project goes perfectly, there's no reason for anyone to feel defensive. Again, the objective of contracting for candor is to put people in a spot where as soon as their reptile brain starts to detect a personal attack, their executive function steps in and says, "Wait a second. This is just something predictable that we agreed to do."

Know When to "LHB." When Tanya was growing up, her grandmother, Joan, had a code at the dinner table: FHB. It stood for Family Hold Back. It meant: "Let our guests serve themselves first to ensure they have plenty to eat."

Similarly, LHB stands for Leader Hold Back. This is something that a pharma exec told us she'd learned to practice. "One time I didn't agree with my R&D head and he said, 'You will come to learn that I am right 100 percent of the time,'" she recalls. "I couldn't believe someone would say that." So, this exec resolved that she would never be a leader who stifles discourse.

But then a few years ago in a 360° feedback profile she was told that she's too quick to give her opinion and it stifled other people from speaking. "So now," the pharma exec says, "I try to hold back and wait for other people to give their opinions before I give mine so that I can hear other options. I've really made an effort to be more of a listener."

Nudge the Narrative. Here are four important things we know about humans and stories:

1. Humans are natural storytellers. We seem to be hardwired to create narratives to explain why things happen and to make sense of our lives.[15]

2. The upside of stories as a means of information sharing is that they are memorable and emotionally engaging. The downside is that, often, they are not very accurate in their depiction of cause and effect. Out of necessity, stories focus on certain details at the expense of others and leave out many relevant facts. Accordingly, the narratives we tell ourselves and each other tend to reflect "deception, blind-spots, wishful thinking, the desire to please or manipulate an audience, lapses of memory, [and] confusion."[16]

3. We tend to create stories that are narcissistic and self-serving. We favor narratives that make us look good by putting us, and our unfailingly noble motives, at the center of the action.

4. We also have a powerful tendency to collude with each other to create stories that protect ourselves when mistakes happen. In nuclear power plants, for example, researchers have found that "when people fail, they tend to be candid about what happened for a short period of time, and then they get their stories straight in ways that justify their actions and protect their reputations. And when official stories get straightened out and get repeated, learning stops."[17]

Recognizing our penchant for self-serving storytelling, effective leaders nudge the narrative, inviting their people to tell stories that are more accurate—and more likely to capture important learnings and practical value when they are remembered and repeated later. Let's tell you how Steve Ambrose does it. Steve is the CIO at DTE, but when he's not in the office you might find him coaching a high school robotics team.

The team is comprised of about 20 students who (using money they've raised themselves) design and build a robot for a specific task; for example, moving balls into a goal or stacking innertubes on a rack. Then they come together in tournaments where they compete head-to-head, in a controlled setting, with as many as 40 other teams (and robots) from across the state of Michigan.

At one competition, the team that Steve mentors performed well in qualifying events over two days, earning them a spot in the finals. This is what they came for. The tournament was theirs to lose.

But in 15 crucial seconds of the competition, Samsung pushed an update to the Android phone the team was using as one of its control devices on their robot. A temporarily unresponsive robot cost them the outcome they'd worked so hard to achieve.

After the disappointing loss, Steve led the team in an after-action review, just like he does after every event (win or lose). It's a detailed discussion of what the team intended, what went well, and what they could do better.

The team's initial response to the last question was "nothing." After all, they said, "we can't control when Samsung sends updates to phones." They were already telling themselves a story that chalked up the loss to just one simple cause: terrible luck.

Steve nudged the narrative by asking questions to see if he could re-center their "locus of control." This term refers to:

> The extent to which people believe they have power over events in their lives. A person with an *internal locus of control* believes that he or she can influence events and their outcomes, while someone with an *external locus of control* blames outside forces for everything.[18]

In this case, Steve began by acknowledging the undeniably unfortunate timing of the phone update. But then he asked: "What could we do so that we're not a victim of this situation in the future?" With that nudge, the team generated some constructive answers, such as: "We can make sure the phones are up to date before the match (because Samsung doesn't push updates to the phone the first day that they are available)." And "We can turn off automatic updates on the phone." In other words, a nudged narrative re-established an internal locus of control and produced practical insights the team could build into their future pre-game checklists.

Before another event, the team found an innovative way to read the rules that, if implemented, would give their robot a small competitive advantage.

As they were setting up for the competition, however, the referee walked over and said, "I don't think you can do that." They weren't allowed to implement their innovation.

Later, in the after-action review, the team complained about the referee, over whom they had no control. Again, Steve nudged the narrative: "What could we do so that we're not a victim of this situation in the future?" And that conversation again produced constructive answers. Before their next competition, the team proactively brought to the referee a written ruling from National Headquarters in New Hampshire that explicitly approved the innovative reading of the rules. The team said to the referee, "We're planning to deploy this. We wanted you to know in advance. Please let us know if you have any questions." The use was allowed, and they got a competitive advantage from deploying it.

Steve says that nudging the narrative is equally important inside the IT organization he leads. "It's a complex, regulated environment, and we deal with lots of 'gravity issues,' factors outside our control. But you can acknowledge the force of gravity and not be its victim. We perform more effectively when we tell ourselves stories that reflect that assumption."

Generously Interpret Motives. Can you confront bad behavior without triggering defensiveness? There are no guarantees, but the odds are a whole lot better if you go into the conversation with curiosity, generously interpreting motives.

An example: You've just learned that Rachel, a member of your team, has made a decision about how to staff a major initiative without consulting you first. What's your intuitive read on the situation? Is it: "That's sneaky and disrespectful. She's a problem." Or are you more likely to consider a more generous interpretation of her motives? As in: "Is it possible she doesn't understand that I've got to be consulted in these kinds of situations?"

Keep in mind that we're talking only about generosity in your interpretation of Rachel's *motives*. This is not about tolerance of her *behavior*. Regardless of where you come down on her motives, you've got to talk to Rachel to readjust her expectations and make sure that she understands the consequences of failure to comply. The operative question is: *What are you trying to accomplish?* To get her to confess to operating with bad motives—and, by extension, acknowledge a significant character deficit? Good luck with that. The more you prosecute, the more defensive and indignant she's likely to become. And the accompanying drama is sure to create a gratuitous distraction for everyone around. The other option is to focus on a much more practical goal: Reinforcing your expectations and significantly increasing the odds that Rachel's behavior in the future will align with your expectations.

We're not going to prescribe a one-size-fits-every-situation script for going "soft on motives, hard on behavior." But the following five-step approach, which you should adapt to fit your natural style and the needs of the situation, works for many:

1. *Observation.* "Hey Rachel, I see you made a staffing decision without checking in with me first."

2. *Hmmm (curiosity).* "So I'm asking myself: Was I not clear about the requirement? Does she not want me to weigh in? Do we have different ideas about what's at stake? So I thought: Instead of wondering, I should come to you directly."

3. *Ask a question.* "So here I am. What can you tell me?"

4. *Clarify expectations.* "Oh, you didn't know it was a requirement. Yeah, well I'm glad we're having this conversation so that I can clear that up."

5. *Confirm understanding.* "Is there anything in the future that might make this requirement difficult to work with? Good. Thanks for this conversation. I suspect we won't need it again."

And then you've got to hold her accountable. (Unless, of course, you determine through candid conversation that the more agile business move is to let her make her own damn staffing decisions.)

Let 'em laugh…even if it's at you. Why do humans laugh? Researchers have concluded it's a "call sign" that signals comfort (non-defensiveness) and affiliation. Perhaps that's why laughter has also shown to increase a group's puzzle-solving capabilities by 20 percent.[19]

So, if the way you show up in conversation with your team encourages them to laugh that is likely going to help you and your team produce positive outcomes.

And that's true even if, from time to time, the laughter is at your expense. It turns out that vulnerability builds trust. Fifty years ago, the social psychologist Elliot Aronson discovered in his research that when people in positions of superiority commit everyday blunders, it makes them more likable, relatable, and trustworthy. He called this phenomenon the "pratfall effect."[20]

That's why we encourage every leader taking on a new assignment to identify at least one story that illustrates a mistake or hard-won lessons learned. When they share this story during their First 100 Days in the new role, it may (depending on the story and how you tell it) evoke smiles while demonstrating vulnerability, thereby promoting affiliation and likeability.

Here's one such story told by an executive whom we coached:

> I took on a new IT job with a high-end retailer. Before I got there, the staff wanted to set everything up and worked hard to organize for me. They dug through drawers and cabinets to prepare specific files that would help me get up to speed.
>
> When I began moving into my new office, I saw this stack of folders sitting on my desk. I thought, "Hmm, what are these doing out?" and I put them back into drawers with the rest of the files. I had a glass-walled office and I noticed people looking in at me with a look of alarm in their eyes as a I put the folders away. But I didn't realize what I'd done until it was too

late—they'd really spent a lot of time preparing these files for me and I really needed them to do my job. They had important phone numbers, strategies, inventory, and marketing plans for all the stores.

Every time he takes on a new role (and he's been promoted more than a few times in the past two decades) he tells his new team the story. They laugh. And he adds: "It's possible that, unintentionally, I'm going to do the equivalent of 'putting file folders away' in this new role. Will you do me a favor and point it out?" That's the vulnerability and "contracting for candor" that really builds trust—and earns him the benefit of the doubt the first time he screws up.

But you don't have to be in your First 100 Days to change the conversation by owning mistakes. Dale Vines, whom you met early in the chapter, was running a Maintenance organization at a large plant when he got a call from Operations about concerns they had on the life expectancy of some brushes in one of their motor generators.

Dale talked to some of his team and concluded it was going to be tough to get to it that day and the team was already scheduled to take care of it the following Tuesday. So they punted it off to the next week. Unfortunately, the machine had other ideas, because it shut down Sunday morning causing a significant business disruption and loss of revenue.

A while later, Dale got the opportunity to stand in front of an all-hands Maintenance Department meeting and explain what had happened. He started it off simply and directly: "Let me walk you through a decision that I made. I own it. I'm accountable for it. The thing is, while it's my mistake, there are things we all can learn from it. And the key thing to learn is that we need to always challenge one another."

An administrative assistant came up to him right after the meeting and asked: "What were you thinking? No leader around here ever says anything is their fault." But the thing is, Dale says, "it *was* my fault. I could have blamed others who had input into the decision, but I was the person who made the final call." Afterward, he got razzed frequently in the cafeteria or out in the field with "Hey, you make any more stupid decisions today?" But he was completely comfortable with it. "That's just how folks in Maintenance show they like you," Dale says. Most importantly, the team made fewer mistakes after that, because they felt more at ease challenging one another. "And when we did make mistakes," Dale says, "we learned more from them, because folks knew it was safe to talk about them and own up to what we could have done better."

Reframe the game. If you've worked with us, you know there are at least three phrases we tend to use a lot—and the reason is that all three of them invite reappraisal of potentially triggering information, which, in turn, promotes Zen Information Flow.

Let's reserve the right to get smarter. We picked up this phrase many years ago from Cliff Dodd, a CIO who'd worked at several different large companies. Cliff wanted to discourage people from stubbornly adhering to a previous decision or position, simply to avoid being seen as "wrong" or a "flip-flopper."

He would say, "If it is not working or it's breaking, just stand up and say, 'You know what? My first decision may have been reasonably correct for what I knew then, but I know a little bit more now, so I reserve the right to get a little smarter.'" As Cliff told us, agility depends on employees embracing this frame: "In an environment where we're reserving the right to get smarter, we're doing two things. First, I'm holding people accountable to make a decision. And second, I'm also holding people accountable to keep getting better."

Don't Ask Who, Ask Why. We picked up this phrase from Jack Brennan, former CEO of Vanguard, though he didn't originate it. "We're always trying to do things better on behalf of our clients," Jack told us. "But the way we do that is not by pointing fingers or assessing blame." Instead, ask "Why aren't we doing as well as we can? Where are the opportunities to improve? And what are the opportunities to capitalize on businesses that we can build?"

As we've noted a few times now, people use excuses as rapid-deploy defenses of their egos and identities. Accordingly, in an organizational culture in which the default reaction to failure is pointing fingers and assigning blame, it should surprise no one when employees devote their best thinking and finite energy to crafting a narrative that minimizes their responsibility. Jack believed (and of course we agree) that by focusing the response to problems and failures predominantly on *why*, not *who*, you can promote a culture in which employees take pride in learning from their mistakes and solving problems.

As a bit of an aside, here's another interesting thing Jack Brennan did to change the conversation at Vanguard: He appointed teams of officers to debate opposite sides of a key business decision under consideration. The side to which they were assigned didn't necessarily align with their actual beliefs. This promoted candor while depersonalizing the debate—so participants were more likely to focus on substance versus *who* held what positions. And in true Aristotelian fashion, these debates revealed truths. "Some of our best decisions came out of these sessions," Jack told us.

Let's treat mistakes as intellectual capital. The ultimate form of reappraisal is to strip all the stigma from mistakes and failures. And then be able to learn from them—dispassionately, or even better, proudly—as a source of business intelligence.

Framing mistakes as intellectual capital goes a long way toward that goal. We picked up this phrase from Walt Buckley, chairman and CEO of Internet Capital Group (ICG). At the height of the Internet boom, ICG's market capitalization exceeded GM's. When the crash eventually came, it hit hard. Instead of blaming everything on forces outside their control (namely, the dot-com crash), Buckley led his team in meditating on their mistakes.

"We had to be honest with ourselves about the mistakes we'd made that put us in that place, including the mistakes I made," Walt told us. "But with the tough lessons came an interesting perspective. Think about it: You make every mistake possible, and you're still around to fight another day? For a band of warriors, that's a liberating feeling." Working from that frame, Buckley created an environment where, without being paralyzed by defensiveness, he and his team could thoughtfully, even proudly, catalog their mistakes, treat them as "intellectual capital," and apply them in their return to battle. "As we headed up the next hill, we turned every one of those mistakes into a guide for how to climb back up to the top," Buckley says.

From Ahmad Tarsin, an IT leader at DTE, we picked up what might be a superior version of the same frame. Ahmad was visiting his son's elementary school classroom when he saw a poster that read: "Mistakes are expected, inspected, and corrected." It would inspire confidence in the future to know that kids are learning and applying this principle.

Actually, young people are leading the way, though they're using language inappropriate for elementary school classrooms. In Mexico City a few years ago, Leticia Gasca and a few other young entrepreneurs, over drinks, spent the evening talking about their mistakes and failures. "We shared our stories for three hours and realized we just had the most meaningful business conversations ever," she recalls.[21] It inspired an idea they call F*ckUp Nights (our asterisk), a TedTalk-ish forum where speakers each get seven minutes to talk about a failure. The concept took off. Today, hundreds of cities on six continents regularly host these events. More than 100,000 people attended a F*ckUp Night event last year. A growing number of companies are licensing the event for in-house use.[22] And Leticia has now created a spin-off, the Failure Institute, to synthesize the powerful insights that this Zen Information Flow is producing.

Ask questions and then listen

Let's go back to Beth M. Foley, the Chief Communications Officer at Edison International we referenced earlier in this chapter. In her first 90 days in her current role, she met with more than 90 people in 1:1 meetings, and a great deal more in group settings. The agenda was simple and the lead-in question broad: "What's going on with you?"

"That simple question often opens the floodgates," she says. The next step is crucial: follow-up. "I like to have coffee meetings to keep the conversation going. If calendars don't allow for that, and often they don't, brief calls, texts or handwritten notes get the job done." Does it take a lot of effort? "Of course," she says. "And, to me, that's the privilege and responsibility of being a leader."

Here are some other questions leaders have found helpful:

- Where are you making progress? What are you proud of or feeling good about?

- What challenges are you facing? Where are you stuck? What could be working better?

- Anyone I should be sure to recognize this week (for his or her hard work, living our values, progress, etc.)?

- What's something cool or positive that's happening outside the spotlight that deserves more attention?

- What's something useful you've learned recently (even if it was from a mistake)?

- What's something small we could be doing now that might have a big impact down the road?

- Anything I need to know but probably don't?

Here's what leaders tell us about that last question: It feels awkward to ask it, at least initially. Often, it produces no response. And sometimes it produces a response only after an awkward silence. But when it does? "Oh, my goodness, I am so glad I asked that question" is something we hear from leaders all the time.

Signal Boost Summary

To turn your culture into a source of competitive advantage, transmit these three Signal Boosts on Frequency 4:

- **Showing up informally starts with showing up, period.** Go where your people go, because that's where they are. Getting out there is an early warning system. Invest the effort to know their names—it's worth the payoff. Take the shoeshine guy (or his equivalent) to lunch. Demonstrate that input about how to improve performance is your priority. And suffer with them, if needed, to demonstrate you are in-tribe.

- **Relinquish your raft.** Honor the Reactive Tendencies that helped bring your leadership journey this far. And then consider upgrading your "Operating System" so you focus less on proving yourself and more on creating outcomes that truly matter to you and others. The impact on how you show up on Frequency 4? Huge.

- **Change the conversation.** "Everything that happens in an organization happens in or because of a conversation." If you want to change the culture, you've got to change the conversation. Practice Zen Information Flow, where anyone can talk to anyone…and fear and egos don't get in the way of solving problems. Contract for candor. Nudge the narrative toward more self-authorship (away from victimhood). Generously interpret motives, so you go soft on intentions and tough on behavior. Show your vulnerability…because it elevates trust. Reserve the right to get smarter. Don't ask who, ask why. Take the stigma out of F*ckUps, so you can treat mistakes as intellectual capital.

FIVE FREQUENCIES

Frequency 5: Formal communications

This chapter covers eight signal boosts for turning culture into competitive advantage

- **Approach strategic alignment as a storytelling exercise**
- **Go past the "puke point"**
- **Shape and perpetuate folklore**
- **Go organic**
- **Don't flood the marketplace**
- **Use Frequency 5 signals to boost Frequency 4**
- **Don't push your people to the black market**
- **Focus your internal communications staff on outcomes, not outputs**

Formal communications is the *last* of the Five Frequencies. Is it also the *least important?*

In some ways, yes. You can't meaningfully change culture on this frequency alone, though many have tried. As Richard Smith, former Realogy CEO, told us, "Treating culture seriously isn't about a program with a banner hanging somewhere. The superficial approaches fail." Indeed, if you transmit one set of signals on Frequencies 1-4 and another set of signals on Frequency 5, your employees will ignore your formal communications—or worse—mock and deride them.

On the other hand, when formal communication is done right, it powerfully amplifies all of your other culture-shifting signals. And that's hardly unimportant!

The big challenge with formal communication is **competing for attention**. As social scientist Herbert Simon observed decades ago, attention is a scarce resource. And therefore, he said in 1971, "a wealth of information creates a poverty of attention."[1] Now think about how much worse that poverty is today! Thousands of new information sources compete against you daily for your employees' finite attention. The average person checks their devices more than 150 times per day.[2] According to a recent Deloitte study, 65 percent of executives rated the "overwhelmed employee" an "urgent" or "important" trend.

All of which raises the question: In a highly competitive and increasingly noisy and chaotic information marketplace, how do you get your employees to *pay* attention?

In the rest of this chapter, we'll prescribe our answers in the form of eight signals boosts.

Signal Boost #1: Approach strategic alignment as a storytelling exercise

Our brains are hardwired for stories. That's why information presented in a recognizable archetype form is more memorable and emotionally resonant. The most common archetype is the quest. According to Christopher Booker in *The Seven Basic Plots*,[3] a quest narrative entails a protagonist and companions setting out to acquire an important object or get to a particular destination. So one of the easiest, most compelling ways to earn employees' attention is to relate a consistent storyline about "where we're going, how we're going to get there," and the role that each employee plays in reaching the destination.

Here's how that worked at the Detroit Water and Sewer Department (DWSD): Gary Brown was a former deputy police chief who, as a whistleblower, helped take down a corrupt Mayor. Later he became President Pro Tem of Detroit's City Council and then the City's Chief Operating Officer. When he agreed to take over DWSD, he recognized he was leading a workforce that performed tough jobs and, coming through Detroit's bankruptcy, they had been through a lot. Now he needed them to help him transform the department. As Gary's boss, Mayor Mike Duggan, said to the Financial Times:[4]

> People get into public service because something in
> their heart wants them to help people, and over time

the bureaucracy beats that idealism out of them. We are trying to bring [idealism] back...If each individual person says, OK my job is to get the grass cut in the parks; my job is to get the tractors repaired 20 per cent faster...turnaround occurs. Not because one or two leaders do some brilliant thing—turnaround occurs when everybody in the organization performs better.

Gary set out to apply this principle at the Water and Sewer Department. He recognized that if he was going to successfully rally and align hundreds of employees behind his turnaround ambitions, he'd need to capture their attention first.

So he began by describing the quest: He wanted DWSD to be an asset in the city's efforts to attract and retain people and businesses (after a half-century of population decline). How would they get there? By focusing on five priorities:

- Putting health and safety first
- Strengthening assets (people, infrastructure)
- Enhancing the customer experience
- Keeping rates fair and affordable
- Making Detroit green

That was the quest. But to truly pull people into the narrative, Gary needed to give them line of sight. To that end, we helped Gary cascade one-page plans to his front-line teams. On these plans, every leader at every level identified their top goals that supported one or more of Gary's five priorities.

Then we used Compass Conversations™ to help everyone see how they contributed. As the name implies, Compass Conversations are about getting everyone pointed in the *same* direction, the *right* direction. As these conversations cascaded throughout the organization, leaders at every level engaged their direct reports around the "where we're going and how we'll get there" storyline. They also reviewed their one-page plan, which described their team's role in making the journey happen. They talked about what they were proud to be doing already that was moving the quest forward. And they talked about what else they could do to advance the righteous cause. Afterward, each team leader provided Gary with feedback about the conversation.

Team leaders said their employees very much appreciated seeing a direct line of sight to an important long-term outcome. Examples:

- "They all feel it's a great idea we are truly trying to get on the same page."

- "My team is excited that we are trying to do something better as a whole."

They also appreciated Gary's interest in hearing what they were already proud to be doing to advance the journey. Examples:

- "We've installed 18 miles of water main and rehabbed 10 miles of sewer. That supports at least four of the five priorities."

- "The team is proud of helping to enhance the customer experience and strengthening DWSD's reputation. We've done this by stepping up our capabilities to educate customers on water-related issues."

(By the way, the long list of things employees were proud of became material for other formal communications.)

Most important, team leaders captured commitments for moving the journey forward. Examples:

- "We're working with the Fire Department to update information on fire hydrants so that they have more accurate information in the field."

- "We're developing ways to implement these programs without causing the need for additional funding to support them."

- "We all feel as though the plans are ambitious and so we will try some things we have not tried before, like using the midnight crew to perform the sounding/leak detection so we can launch this preventive maintenance program."

Overall, the feedback showed that Gary's Compass Conversation successfully pulled his people into the narrative. But how could he keep them there? That's where Progress Huddles come in. According to research conducted by Harvard Business School Professor Teresa Amabile:[5]

> Of all the things that can boost emotions, motivation, and perceptions during a workday, the single most important is making progress in meaningful work. And the more frequently people experience that sense of progress, the more likely they are to be creatively productive in the long run. Whether they are trying to solve a major scientific mystery or simply produce a high-quality product or service, everyday progress—

even a small win—can make all the difference in how they feel and perform.

Designed with this principle in mind, Progress Huddles are regular, leader-led conversations where teams step back from the day-to-day grind and look at their performance relative to their goals and targets. Where they are on track, they celebrate. Where they aren't, they collaboratively problem solve what it will take to get that way. When people see sustained focus and momentum, it perpetuates more of the same. As Gary is first to attest, the DWSD still has a long way to go on its quest—but they've already come a long way.

Signal Boost #2: Go past the "puke point"

Many years ago, we helped a senior leader at a well-known insurance company craft the storyline around which he planned to rally, align, and engage thousands of employees. Part of the rollout strategy involved the senior leader conducting town halls across the company to share the message and answer questions. Because it was so important to get employees on board, we put in place a measurement system (based on employee survey data) to track progress.

After a few town halls, the leader asked: "Are we there yet? Do employees understand and embrace the strategy?" Not yet, we said.

After a few more town halls, same question, same response: Not yet.

After a few more town halls, the senior leader was exasperated. "I'm so tired of hearing myself deliver the same message. In fact, if I have to do this one more time, I think I'm going to puke."

We were happy to report that we had just tracked a spike in employees' understanding the new strategy, believing it was the right strategy, and feeling like their leaders were genuinely committed to it. But to sustain the progress, we urged him to continue to stay on message, past his puke point.

We've seen this phenomenon play out in other organizations as well. It's remarkable how often the "lose your lunch" moment coincides with an upswing in employee understanding of and engagement around the strategy. In other words, it's critical to stay on message even after you're sick of hearing yourself say the same thing—because that's often the turning point where employees are just starting to truly "get it."

Signal Boost #3: Shape and perpetuate folklore

You can learn a lot about an organization and its culture by its folklore—the stories about the past that are best remembered and most-often repeated. Here's a great example: If you go to work at DTE, the largest provider of electricity and gas service in Michigan, you won't be there a week before you hear from your new colleagues a story about what happened during the Great Recession.

As everyone knows, Detroit really took a hit. The automakers, everybody, was laying off thousands of employees. But DTE CEO

Gerry Anderson resisted following suit. Instead, he went to his 10,000 employees and said: "I don't want anyone to lose their job. But the only way to avoid that is if we find $200 million in cost savings. If we work together on continuous improvement, we can do it." And they did. Union employees, management employees, everyone came together to work smarter and find the cost savings. No layoffs. The company not only survived but began to thrive.

Like we said, your folklore says a lot about your culture. In DTE's case, this story tells you about the company's "we all stick together" mentality (which is not to be taken for granted in a workforce that is about 50 percent unionized). It tells you about the company's commitment to being a force for growth in Michigan by taking a risk to avoid contributing to the local economy's job losses. And it tells you about the central importance of continuous improvement to the company's "operating system."

This story is so powerful, it has largely perpetuated itself at DTE.

But in other settings, it doesn't hurt to shape and perpetuate folklore by design. For example, at Nike:[6]

> Buildings and roads are named for [the company's] "founding fathers." … [Senior executives] tell the story of Phil Knight selling running shoes out of the trunk of his Plymouth Valiant. They tell the story of the magic waffle iron [the kitchen appliance ruined in the company's first R&D effort]. They tell the story of Steve Prefontaine, the legendary Oregon runner who died in a car crash and who Knight speaks about in almost spiritual reverence. The heroics of the past inspire the innovations of the future.

This kind of large-scale, systemized folklore can be powerful. But the simpler, more routine way to shape and perpetuate folklore is to use formal communications to make heroes out of the individuals and teams who are doing what's needed. They key is storytelling that puts people and teams at the center of the action. Here's an example:

"When you're trying to improve plant performance, you've got to deliberately reinforce the behaviors and performance you want to see more of," says Pete Sena, President of PSEG Nuclear. "Early in the turnaround efforts at one plant, a group of electricians did a really nice job on a maintenance challenge. They found the problems, fixed them, and brought us back on schedule. No errors. I said to our communications team: 'Write an article and get a picture.' The article came out and it was good. The picture was of…the *fixed equipment*. Missed opportunity. If you want to motivate people, don't showcase equipment, showcase people!"

Pete is right. You can amplify your culture-shifting signals on Frequency 2 by making folk heroes out of high performers and high performances on Frequency 5. The high performers get a reinforcing warm signal and the rest of the organization gets a message about what's valued. And, they're more likely to pay attention to and repeat the message to others, since it's delivered in a memorable and emotionally resonant "package."

Jeff Rocke, who's served as a communications leader for several major companies, recalls a hospital system president he supported earlier in his career who turned making higher performers into folk heroes an art.

We created a recognition program called Everyday Heroes to recognize the people who were doing great things across the region. We gathered their stories and featured them in "galleries" across the lobbies of our hospitals and administration buildings. Then the president took it to the next level with a personal "road tour" from San Diego to San Francisco in a 37-foot RV. We stopped at eight facilities over four days and he led personal and public recognition of our Everyday Heroes in the break rooms and hallways of hospitals and medical offices. It was a huge hit. The next year we did another road tour, this time from north to south, going to different facilities. Over this same period, our culture measurably strengthened. And as engagement improved, so did the care to our members, their patients, and families.

Of course, you don't need to rent a Winnebago to make folk heroes out of high performers. You need only to look for stories of people demonstrating the behavior you want to see more of, especially when it's not easy for them to do so. And then seize every opportunity to retell those stories, even if the featured high performer isn't in the audience. They'll get another reinforcing warm signal when someone who *was* in the audience tells them about it.

Signal Boost #4: Go organic

In many organizations, the amount of attention that employees will pay to any new thing that leaders introduce is inversely proportional to how much the thing is accompanied by "initiative branding," new acronyms and jargon, splash, gloss, or esoteric and self-important language (for example, the use of the verb "strive," which practically no one uses in day-to-day conversation). In reality, low-hype, high-substance communication using organic language competes for attention best.

As Axios' Jim Vandehei puts it:[7]

> What all employees — millennials in particular — want to know is what you're doing and why you're doing it. So just say it that way. Social media thankfully forces authenticity and writing like you would speak in normal settings. Your "what" and "why" should be in this casual language. If you sound like a corporate robot, reboot.

Here's an example of one such reboot: At one client organization, the company president wrote a column each week on an important topic, which was posted to the intranet. The columns averaged 8-10 paragraphs. While the president chose the topic each week, a very good executive speechwriter wrote the actual content. So it was always well-written and even reflected the leader's voice. But it's unlikely that many of the organization's 20,000 employees believed that their senior leader was sitting at his laptop banging out polished paragraphs every week. Which might help to explain the disappointing readership: Metrics showed that only 10 percent of employees clicked on the column each week.

We suggested that the leader switch to a blog, with shorter posts (one, maybe two, breezy, conversational paragraphs), a few times per week. Additionally, the leader made and posted short videos, most of them shot with his own iPad, in which he answered questions that employees sent him. Nothing slick. Nothing polished. Readership quickly quadrupled.

Signal Boost #5: Don't flood the marketplace

Leaders can't expect employees to pick out and pay attention to their genuinely important messages if they've flooded the informational marketplace with cheap imitations. But lots of organizations push out communications to their employees like a Soviet factory—uncoordinated, undisciplined, and without regard to the actual demand or need for what it's producing. This misguided activity often flows from good intentions: "We just did something. And it's important to communicate. Ergo, let's communicate what we just did."

In other cases, leaders make supply-side communication choices for narcissistic reasons, because it makes them feel good; for example, to show off all the important stuff they're doing: "I just got asked to lead an important initiative that will have a meaningful enterprise-wide impact two years from now. Everyone must understand that NOW!" Never mind the absence of any business case for producing that awareness.

In other cases, excess communication supply follows excess production capacity: "We have an expensive editing suite, so for goodness sake let's make some videos."

In any case, uncoordinated, undisciplined, supply-side communication choices—instead of producing "fully informed employees"—create an environment where employees just ignore most of the information delivered through formal channels while wondering what is really happening…and what messages they really ought to align with and pay attention to. This undermines leaders' ability to get their people engaged around efforts to promote the organization's long-term business and reputational interests.

What's the alternative? Coordinated, disciplined, demand-driven communication practices. Tight message discipline. Embracing "less is more." Recognizing that every message of secondary importance has the potential to diminish a message of primary importance—and therefore, deciding to keep it out of the organization's information marketplace may be the best decision.

Signal Boost #6: Use Frequency 5 signals to boost Frequency 4

In the vast majority of organizations, four-fifths of employees identify their immediate leader as their preferred information source. And yet too many organizations ineffectively equip managers and supervisors for this role. Others make the most of this important communication asset by equipping front-line leaders with privileged and prioritized information on Frequency 5 (formal communication) that these leaders can then credibly deliver via informal conversations (Frequency 4).

What does it mean to equip front-line leaders with privileged and prioritized information?

- **Privileged information:** Front-line leaders are almost always communicating with their employees. But if you're treating them as just information "pass-throughs," they're probably not communicating what you want them to. In our research of this important audience, they tell us they feel resentful, under-utilized, and ill-informed when they're expected to simply "hit the forward button," or read information off a sheet of paper. They don't want to look like parrots. What they do want is to look smart, relevant, and ready to translate higher-level messages at the local level. They want to be prepared for the toughest questions their employees might ask. This means using all-leader meetings, skip-level meetings, structured cascade processes, and BS-free leader materials that explain the "why," not just the "what" we're doing. Additionally, it's valuable to provide a "single source of truth"—a place where leaders can pull information when they need it. In order to be useful, however, it must be updated and current, easy to navigate, and user-friendly.

- **Prioritized information:** In a crowded information marketplace, leaders struggle with information overload—even when they believe that all the information is valuable. The solution is to (1) *streamline* communication so front-line leaders have fewer sources to monitor; (2) *filter* the information so leaders get more of "what's relevant to me," and less of the other stuff; and then (3) *prioritize* what you need and expect them to communicate. They'd rather you say—*"This communication is the priority this week"*—than to guess which one of 15 messages is most important. To that end, we've helped organizations successfully put in place a governed process for pushing, on a regular cadence, a *finite* number of prioritized messages to front-line leaders. For example, every two weeks there are only two corporate messages, two business unit messages, and two local messages the company requires front-line leaders to deliver effectively. With clear and credible expectations in place, these companies then create positive consequences for the managers and supervisors who play their communication role effectively, and negative consequences for those who don't.

Signal Boost #7: Don't push your people to the black market

Some of the toughest competition for your employees' attention comes from the rumor mill. This is especially true in the midst of uncertainty. Unfortunately, this is when many leaders withdraw from the communication marketplace—waiting until everything is finalized. To compete for attention, you can't do that.

Instead, communicating probabilities is a very good practice. Introduced by TJ and Sandar Larkin in their seminal work, *Communicating Change,*[8] communicating probabilities means equipping employees with the current thinking about what is definitely going to happen, what is probably going to happen, what is truly uncertain, what is probably not going to happen, and what is definitely not going to happen. To many leaders it sounds counter-intuitive to talk about what isn't certain. But it makes perfect sense from an economic perspective. In the midst of change, people in the organization want to reduce their uncertainty. So if leaders don't provide an alternative, employees will turn to the black market (the rumor mill) for information to fill that need. Often, the rumor mill spins out inaccurate or exaggerated information—but if it's the only thing available, there's a market for it. And when they're no longer paying attention to their organization's leadership, it's difficult to rally them around a call to action.

Here's an example of a probabilities fact sheet that one of our clients distributed to front-line leaders in the midst of uncertainty and change. (It's an example of providing front-line leaders privileged information and equipping them as preferred information channels on Frequency 4, as described above). Leaders, in turn, are responsible for diffusing the information to employees.

What can employees expect?

As you know, we're undergoing significant change this year. While we don't know everything that's going to happen, if we hold back information until everything is certain, you'll never hear anything. So, based on current information, this is what we expect...

Will happen:
- Our organization will become smaller than it is now
- Fewer local investment projects (due to greater investment in national initiatives)
- Demand for skillsets will change, with greater demand for integration skills

- Skill assessment and development
- We'll implement new practices, processes, and rigor to increase productivity and improve product quality
- We'll recognize and reward top performers
- We'll identify poor performers; they'll improve their performance or find work elsewhere

Probably will happen:

- Further realignment of staff with other functional organizations
- Further leadership and management changes as the next year unfolds

What's uncertain:

- How much smaller the organization will be than it is now…and when those changes will occur
- Whether we'll need to ask a small number of employees to relocate

Won't happen:

- Large-scale relocation
- Off-shoring or outsourcing of our entire operation

The client updated the fact sheet every few weeks as the situation changed and new information needs emerged. Even when employees didn't like some of the changes, they appreciated getting reliable, uncertainty-reducing information from a preferred information source.

Signal Boost #8: Focus your internal communications staff on out*comes*, not *outputs*

Historically, leaders in large organizations have looked to the internal communication function to play a primarily tactical role, focused on delivering formal communication *products* "to specs." In this model, the employee communication department is an internal vendor. Communicators provide value and make names for themselves based on their writing, editing, event management, and production skills, as well as their proficiency in the latest communication tools and social media. What gets measured is activity ("How many videos did we produce?") and attention ("How many people visited our news page on the intranet site last week?").

The alternative—one that provides significantly more value—is to focus on out*comes* before focusing on out*put*. What outcomes?

Starting on the next page, in our wrap-up chapter, we'll describe how the Five Frequencies fit into a larger framework for turning culture into competitive advantage. It starts with measurably defining your desired-state culture, measuring the gaps between current- and desired-state culture, and then using strong and steady signals across the Five Frequencies to close those gaps. So when we say you should focus internal communications staff on out*comes*, we're talking about harnessing their talents and capabilities to help you move the needle on culture. Cool new communication products, events, and technologies, when used, are merely a means to an end. Never for their own sake.

Signal Boost Summary

Want to turn your culture into a source of competitive advantage? Here's a recap of eight Signal Boosts on Frequency 5:

- **Approach strategic alignment as a storytelling exercise:** Our brains are hardwired for stories, and one of the easiest, most compelling ways to earn employees' attention is to relate a consistent storyline about "where we're going, how we're going to get there," and the role that each employee plays in reaching the destination.

- **Go past the "puke point":** To sustain the message, you must endure past the point at which you're so tired of hearing yourself speak that you feel you're going to "lose your lunch." This is often the point when employees are just starting to truly "get it."

- **Shape and perpetuate folklore:** Look for people demonstrating the behaviors you want to see more of—and make folk heroes out of them. Tell and retell stories of high performers and high performance.

- **Go organic:** In Frequency 5, less is often more. Less branding, jargon, splash, and fanfare. Low-hype, high-substance communication using organic language competes best for attention.

- **Don't flood the marketplace:** Use coordinated, disciplined, demand-driven communication practices—and tight message discipline. Reduce or eliminate messages of secondary importance, so the ones of primary importance get through.

- **Use Frequency 5 signals to boost Frequency 4:** Equip front-line leaders with privileged and prioritized information on Frequency 5 so they can credibly deliver it on Frequency 4.

- **Don't push your people to the black market:** Communicate probabilities when you don't yet have all of the answers. Otherwise expect the rumor mill to fill the void.

- **Focus your internal communications staff on out*comes*, not out*put*:** Instead of measuring communication activity, measure how well your communication team is helping you close the gap between the culture you have and the culture you need. (More on this in Chapter 6.)

CHAPTER 6

MEASURING AND MANAGING CULTURE

Strong and steady signals on Five Frequencies: That's how you move the needle on culture. But what exactly is the needle measuring? That's where Know / Feel / Do®, the other half of our culture framework, comes into play. In this wrap-up chapter, we'll show you what we mean.

Know / Feel / Do®
- **How you measure culture**

Five Frequencies®
- **How you move the needle**

A few years ago, a nuclear power plant experienced a troubling pattern of reliability and employee safety issues. Plant leaders, the parent company, and regulators all pinpointed the plant's too-tolerant-of-mediocre-performance culture as a root cause. That's when we got involved, to help them run a series of culture-shifting experiments aimed at fixing the problem. There, like everywhere else, we based our experiments on two basic hypotheses:

- *Hypothesis 1*: Stronger and steadier signals across the Five Frequencies will measurably strengthen culture—closing the gap between "the culture you have" and "the culture you need."

- *Hypothesis 2*: When you measurably strengthen culture, business performance will follow.

To test these hypotheses, we first had to measurably define the plant's desired-state culture. We could have measured desired-state culture using the engagement survey regularly conducted across every unit of the parent company. But those twelve, one-size-fits-all questions seemed too blunt a measurement instrument for this job. So, our first task was to help the nuclear plant's leadership team develop a *fit-for-purpose culture metric*.

Measurably defining desired-state culture

How did we do this? There are a lot of different ways that people define culture, but according to many academics, culture manifests itself in employees' cognition, affect, and behavior. As non-academics, we're more frugal with our syllables. So, we say that culture shows up in what employees *know*, what they *feel*, and what they *do*. Know / Feel / Do is the framework we developed for measurably defining desired-state culture.

At the nuclear plant, we pulled the top leaders into a room and said, "Let's talk about a culture here that would make improved plant performance both *possible* and *probable*. In that culture, what do all plant employees consistently know, feel, and do?"

As is typical, they generated over 50 possible answers to the question. But we said, "You can't focus on 50 things. Let's focus on the 12 to 18 things that will make 80+ percent of the difference." After a lot of strenuous, even heated, debate, they ultimately prioritized the 15 Know / Feel / Do items that would comprise the plant's tailored culture metric. Figure 1 highlights some of them.

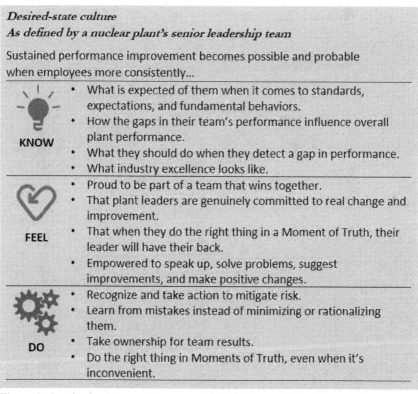

Figure 1: One leadership team's measurable definition of desired-state culture

Capturing a baseline and understanding the gaps

With desired-state culture measurably defined, we needed a baseline measurement to know where plant leaders were starting from in their efforts to shift the culture. We have a few different tools for conducting baseline measurements. But in this case, we used a simple, anonymous employee survey. We translated each of the Know / Feel / Do items into belief statements and we asked employees to rate their agreement with each statement on a 5-point scale.

Surprising to no one, we identified some significant gaps between the plant's current and desired-state culture. For example, too few employees knew how the gaps in their performance impacted overall plant performance. Way too few felt proud to be part of a team that wins together. And they definitely didn't believe plant leadership was committed to real change and improvement. As a result, many weren't doing what they needed to do to lift plant performance. In short, there was lots of work to do to make the plant's culture an asset rather than a liability.

Launching culture-shifting experiments

Using the Five Frequencies as a framework, we supported the senior team as they determined what culture-shifting actions they'd take—plant-wide and within specific departments—to try to move the needle on culture.

Figure 2 highlights some of the things they did:

Strong and Steady Signals Across Five Frequencies

Frequency 1: Decisions and actions

- They moved out some leaders who had helped produce the mediocre culture and performance.
- They invested in facility improvements and equipment purchases and repairs.
- They identified programs and processes they could stop doing— so employees could focus on what mattered most.

Frequency 2: What's rewarded and recognized

- Senior leaders more consistently gave "shout outs" for good performance, strong effort, and teamwork.
- Plant-wide, they created a new and focused recognition program for surfacing problems.
- They celebrated successes and accomplishments.

Frequency 3: What's tolerated (or isn't)

- They increased the rigor in the cadence and structure of daily operations.
- They resolved over 200 industrial safety issues.
- They launched a site-wide, leader-led Moment of Truth exercise (like we described in chapter 3) so that when employees avoided risky shortcuts, even in the midst of time and productivity pressure, they could feel confident that site leadership would have their backs.
- They more consistently corrected ineffective or inappropriate behaviors.

Frequency 4: How leaders show up informally

- They cancelled many standing meetings and then charged leaders with using their newfound time in the field observing and coaching.
- Senior leaders spent more time conducting walk-abouts.

Frequency 5: Formal communications

- They cascaded performance information every week to help ensure employees had more line of sight.
- They used formal communication channels to make folk heroes of the individuals and teams delivering the kind of performance leaders wanted to see more of.

Figure 2: Examples of culture-shifting actions that moved the needle

Post-test measurements, learning, recalibration

Five months later, we conducted a post-test measurement to see whether and how much the leaders' strong and steady signals across the Five Frequencies had moved the needle on culture. Scores for every Know / Feel / Do item went up—across management, represented, and non-represented employees. In fact, every feel score increased significantly. There was still plenty of room for improvement, but there was momentum. We met again with the senior team, and then with each of the department teams, to debrief their post-test results. Together, we extracted learnings from the data. And then they updated their culture-shifting experiments for the following period, doubling down on what was working and recalibrating what wasn't.

This cycle of leaders working their signals, then measuring culture, extracting learnings, and recalibrating culture-shifting plans every 5 or 6 months, continued.

18 Months Later…

…it seemed like a different plant. All the culture scores had improved significantly. The average scores moved from 2s and 3s to 4s on a 5-point scale. The most dramatic spike? The vast majority of employees now *felt* confident that leaders were genuinely committed to real change and improvement. The 1.4-point lift on that item was among the largest we measured anywhere that year.

But we don't give out trophies to the clients with the most impressive scores. We believe that measurably strengthening culture, when it lifts business performance, is its own reward.

And that's what happened at this nuclear plant: Their Know / Feel / Do culture metric proved to be a reliable leading indicator of actual business performance. The plant experienced the best refueling outage in plant history (the previous one had been the worst); they enjoyed the best safety record in plant history; and they increased electricity output.

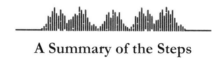

A Summary of the Steps

Let's recap the primary steps in the process.

Measurably Define Desired-State Culture. Your definition should be fit-for-purpose, meaning it is strictly rationalized against the business outcomes you have declared. Ask: "What is the culture that makes this outcome *possible* and *probable*? What will employees consistently KNOW? FEEL? DO?" We typically make suggestions and share examples of our Know / Feel / Do models from other organizations. But we don't believe you should outsource in wholesale fashion to any consultant (us included) the definition of your desired-state culture. You own it, we don't.

Establish a baseline so you understand the gaps. We use a few different tools for this. The key is to get the most robust data possible while minimizing survey fatigue and intrusion in the organization. But we will say this: You will more meaningfully understand the gaps between *the culture you have* and *the culture you need* if you gather both quantitative and qualitative data about the current state.

Develop culture-shifting action plans to move the needle on culture. We recommend that leaders make plans collectively (as an intact team) and as individual leaders. And then run these culture-shifting experiments.

Post-test measurements, learning, recalibration. Don't wait more than six months before you get some more data to gauge whether and how you're moving the needle on culture. Extract learnings from the data. What's working? What isn't? Update your culture-shifting plans for the next cycle.

After you've completed two cycles, it's time to examine what at the outset of this chapter we called "Hypothesis 2." If we're measurably strengthening culture, we expect business performance to follow. Are we seeing evidence that this is the case? What can we learn?

As we said in chapter 4: Reserve the right to get smarter! Sometimes it makes sense to update your Know / Feel / Do items as you gather new insights about the culture that's required to produce competitive advantage. There's no shame in sharpening your measurement tool.

Five Things We've Learned

After a lot of years helping senior leaders measure and manage culture for competitive advantage, we've observed a handful of things worth noting.

1. Heated debate is a good thing.

When we're helping a leadership team measurably define their desired-state culture, the conversations often get heated. Leaders put a lot of passion into their arguments for why some Know / Feel / Do items are better than others. On more than one occasion, someone has stormed out of the room.

We don't encourage conflict for its own sake. But we've learned that heated debate is a good thing when you're defining desired-state culture. It creates ownership that sometimes is missing with engagement surveys. When senior leaders get lousy engagement survey results, they sometimes question the metric and its practical business value. (For example: "With everything else going on, is my highest and best use really helping people find a 'best friend at work'?"— referencing one of the classic Gallup questions.) It's not for us to say whether they're right or merely making excuses. Instead, our point is that when senior leaders define for themselves a fit-for-purpose culture metric, it's pretty damned difficult for them to justify data denial even when they hate their survey results.

2. It has got to be clear: Leaders own culture, supported by HR. Not the other way around.

HR, Corporate Communications, and other support functions can provide invaluable support. But if the support functions care more about moving the needle on culture than leaders do, call off the experiment. It won't work. Leaders must steward culture-shifting efforts; it's not something they can delegate.

3. What employees *feel* is more important than what they *know*.

We were helping a senior team at a manufacturing plant measurably define their desired-state culture. One of the leaders spoke up: "Can we just come up with 'know' and 'do' items? This is a tough environment, a union environment. Nobody gives a damn how anybody *feels*."

Our response: "That sentiment is a core part of your problem. And if you give us the opportunity, we'll back up our argument with statistical modeling." They proceeded to use all three parts of the Know / Feel / Do framework to define their desired-state culture. When we got the baseline data, we ran a regression analysis to identify which of the know and feel items were the strongest predictors of employee behavior (what employees do). Three feel items explained 70 percent of the variance. For union employees, what they *felt* proved to be an even stronger predictor of behavior. We've seen this play out again and again when we run similar predictive analyses across many different industries. Even if you're working in an environment where employees typically don't talk about their feelings, their feelings—at least some of those feelings—produce a big impact on how those employees perform.

4. It's easier to go from bad to good than from good to great.

Sometimes we get calls from prospective clients who tell us candidly that their culture is in a really bad place. "Have you ever worked anywhere where it's this grim? Is it actually possible for us to fix our culture?" The good news we can share with them is that, when it comes to culture, many leaders find it easier to go from bad to good than from good to great.

Here's why: When failure is not a viable option, it helps to focus and sustain leadership attention. It frees up resources. But when having a strong culture is merely something you'd *like to have*, rather than what you *need to have*, it's easy to get distracted. The Know / Feel / Do and Five Frequencies framework for measuring and managing culture is simple—but the actual leadership work can be difficult.

Here's a cautionary tale of how this played out in one organization.

The company had two major business units. Let's call them the Blue Unit and the Red Unit. Something really bad happened in Blue Unit that revealed a lousy culture. The parent company brought us in to help them fix it. We asked: Should we just focus on Blue Unit...or make this more of an enterprise-wide effort to strengthen culture (and therefore include Red Unit)? They decided on the latter.

We developed a fit-for-purpose culture metric that applied enterprise-wide. The senior team in Blue Unit, which was undergoing a ton of ongoing scrutiny, took their lousy baseline results very seriously. They built and implemented a robust culture-shifting plan, with strong and steady signals across the Five Frequencies, to move the needle. And then they implemented it. Cycle after cycle, their culture scores continued to improve. And business performance followed.

Meanwhile, the senior team in Red Unit, where there wasn't much scrutiny, seemed to resent having to be involved in this effort. After all, it was Blue Unit that got the company into trouble in the first place. And yet Red Unit's baseline culture scores weren't much better than Blue Unit's. Nonetheless, over a multi-year period, Red Unit leaders expressed minimal interest in their culture metrics and in taking action to move the needle. Not too long after that, the company ran into another big problem, this time originating in Red Unit, and it bankrupted the whole company.

Another cautionary tale: A leadership team did all the right things to turn a bad culture good. And then, despite our protests, prematurely declared victory and decided the culture was good enough. After all, they had a lot going on. They wanted to focus their attention to other things, like operational improvements. A year later it was clear that they'd surrendered many of their hard-earned gains on the culture front (which undermined their efforts to sustain operational improvements).

Culture is like anything else important in your business. To sustain it as a source of competitive advantage, you must first treat it seriously and then continue to do so. Dr. Will Roper, assistant secretary of the U.S. Air Force for acquisition, technology and logistics, recently summarized this point nicely. He was talking to Boeing, critiquing their culture, after the company delivered planes with trash and tools left inside:

> Culture is something that I'm not going to believe because [you] have a good month, or a good two months, that the culture is back. I'm going to believe it when I see month after month for a long time that yes, those practices are now things that aren't just being done because they have to be done, they are being done because the workforce says, "This is a product we deliver to the Air Force."[1]

5. Your capability to move the needle on culture must keep pace with your capability to measure culture.

We've worked with a bunch of organizations where we've observed something utterly insane: They invest in a few cycles of running an enterprise-wide engagement survey—focusing on lifting employee response rates each time—before they turn their attention to getting good at actually acting on the data. Nothing frustrates employees more than continuing to provide the same feedback time after time while nothing changes.

We think it's important to be good at both: Measuring culture…and having mechanisms in place to move the needle. With Know / Feel / Do and Five Frequencies, that's our bread and butter. But if for some reason you were going to over-toggle on one versus the other, we'd suggest you put more emphasis on moving the needle on culture (and then play catch-up on your ability to measure it).

Five Frequencies Fishbone™ Diagrams

We're going to close out the book by equipping you with a tool for assessing how you got the culture you have…and what it will take to produce the culture you need.

You might already have experience with fishbone diagrams as a tool for analysis and continuous improvement. They're sometimes called cause and effect diagrams. That's because the head of the fish represents the "effect" or outcome you're trying to explain. And then you use a handful of "bones" coming off the fish's backbone to theorize the "causes" that produce the outcome.

Use a retrospective Five Frequencies Fishbone to reflect on how you got to the culture you have now. Think of something about the current-state culture that's a liability, a source of competitive *disadvantage*. For illustration, here are some undesirable current state outcomes that other leaders have placed in the fish head of their backward-looking fishbone diagram.

- Millennials don't seem to KNOW the values or guiding principles that should guide their decisions and behaviors.
- Front-line employees don't seem to consistently KNOW how their work supports the vision.
- Many field employees don't FEEL supported and equipped to continuously improve their performance.
- Few employees FEEL they're supported to take informed risks, "fail fast," and learn from mistakes.

- Employees too often don't ask for help when they need it. (DO)

- Mid-managers don't root for each other's success or play to win as a team. (DO)

Now draw the body of your fish with five bones coming off the spines.

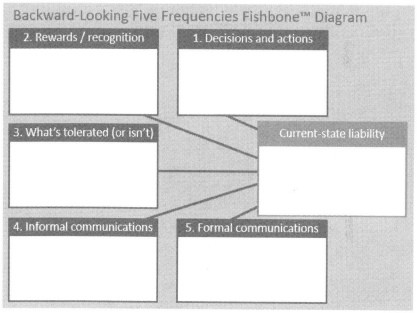

Figure 3: Use this fishbone to identify where current-state culture came from

Now work your way around the Five Frequencies. Looking back over the past few years, what were the signals that you or other leaders transmitted that intentionally—or more likely, unintentionally—produced this outcome? The more candid and self-critical you are, the more helpful the resulting analysis will be. If you need help with the Fishbone analysis, ask your colleagues, or even better, your employees.

When it's complete, the retrospective Fishbone will help you identify what you need to change to get employees to more consistently know, feel, or do what you need them to know, feel, or do.

A prospective Five Frequencies Fishbone looks ahead, helping you theorize what it will take across the Five Frequencies to produce some element of your desired-state culture. Pick something that you need employees to more consistently know, feel, or do. This becomes the head of your fish.

For illustration, here are some desired-state outcomes that other leaders have placed in the fish head of their forward-looking fishbone diagram.

- Employees in the support functions KNOW as well as customer-facing employees how their work contributes to our "North Star."

- New employees KNOW examples of us living our values, even when it's inconvenient.

- Operations employees FEEL increasingly able to get things done with the right resources and processes rather than depending on "personal heroics."

- Team members FEEL local leaders are genuinely committed to our agile transformation.

- Employees DO manage conflict constructively rather than avoiding it or taking it personally.

- Individual contributors DO take charge and are proactive when they see issues.

Then work your way around the Five Frequencies: What signals will you likely need to transmit for your employees to more consistently know, feel, or do what you need them to? Reviewing your notes from reading this book's first five chapters, what signal boosts can you use to strengthen these frequencies? Again, the more candid and self-critical you are, the more helpful the resulting analysis will be. Take your first cut at the analysis, and then invite colleagues and employees to weigh in.

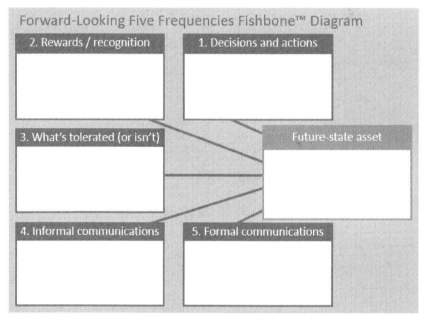

Figure 4: Use this fishbone to assess what it will take to produce the culture you need for competitive advantage

And when your analysis is complete, start sending those signals! Keep 'em strong. Keep 'em steady. Of course, it's not easy—just worth it. Because, as we've seen time and again, when you measurably strengthen culture, business performance follows.

ABOUT THE AUTHORS

Jeff Grimshaw, Tanya Mann, Lynne Viscio, and Jennifer Landis are principals at MGStrategy. For two decades, they've helped leaders measure and manage culture as a source of competitive advantage. First, they help leaders assess the gap between *the culture they have* and *the culture they need*. Then they help leaders close that gap, with strong and steady signal on Five Frequencies. The payoff? When leaders measurably strengthen culture, business performance follows.

Based in Philadelphia, they are currently helping leaders on six continents.

You can find them at www.mgstrat.com.

Notes

Introduction

[1] Bethany McLean and Peter Elkind, The Smartest Guys in the Room: The Amazing Rise and Scandalous Fall of Enron (Portfolio Trade, 2003).

[2] Vito J. Racanelli, "The Winners: Alphabet, Apple, and Amazon.Com," *Barron's*, June 3, 2017, http://www.barrons.com/articles/the-winners-alphabet-apple-and-amazon-com-1496463242.

[3] Bethany McLean, "How Wells Fargo's Cutthroat Corporate Culture Allegedly Drove Bankers to Fraud," *The Hive*, Summer 2017, https://www.vanityfair.com/news/2017/05/wells-fargo-corporate-culture-fraud.

[4] Kristine Phillips, "Warren Buffett Slams Wells Fargo's Handling of Massive Sales Scandal," *Washington Post*, May 7, 2017, https://www.washingtonpost.com/news/business/wp/2017/05/07/warren-buffett-slams-wells-fargos-handling-of-massive-sales-scandal/.

[5] McLean, "How Wells Fargo's Cutthroat Corporate Culture Allegedly Drove Bankers to Fraud."

[6] McLean.

[7] McLean.

[8] Charlie LeDuff, Detroit: An American Autopsy (Penguin Books, 2013).

Chapter 1

[1] Jim VandeHei and Mike Allen, "Trump Creep: Bad Habits Spread Fast," Axios, February 14, 2018, https://www.axios.com/trump-bad-habits-white-house-republicans-congress-87dc1136-b9b1-414e-a951-553bc117cd46.html.

[2] D. Michael Abrashoff, *It's Your Ship: Management Techniques from the Best Damn Ship in the Navy*, 10th Anniversary Revised & Updated edition (New York: Grand Central Publishing, 2012).

[3] Michael Bazigos and Emily Caruso, "Why Frontline Workers Are Disengaged," *McKinsey Quarterly*, March 2016, https://www.mckinsey.com/business-functions/organization/our-insights/why-frontline-workers-are-disengaged.

[4] Nassim Nicholas Taleb, Skin in the Game (p. 219), Incerto (Random House, 2018), https://en.wikipedia.org/w/index.php?title=Skin_in_the_Game_(book)&oldid=880234475.

[5] Lisa Endlich, *Goldman Sachs: The Culture of Success*, Reprint edition (New York, NY: Touchstone, 2000).

[6] Nick Paumgarten, "The Death of Kings," *The New Yorker*, May 18, 2009, https://www.newyorker.com/magazine/2009/05/18/the-death-of-kings-3.

[7] Goldman Sachs: Sorry About The Financial Crisis. (2009, June 17). Retrieved from http://www.businessinsider.com/goldman-sachs-sorry-about-the-financial-crisis-2009-6

[8] Larry Fink, "Larry Fink's Letter to CEOs," BlackRock, n.d., https://www.blackrock.com/corporate/investor-relations/larry-fink-ceo-letter.

[9] Mark Lefko, "How Long-Term Thinking Leads To Sustainable Decisions," *Real Leaders*, December 15, 2016, https://real-leaders.com/long-term-thinking-leads-sustainable-decisions/.

[10] Lefko.

[11] Adi Ignatius, "Jeff Bezos on Leading for the Long-Term at Amazon," *Harvard Business Review*, n.d., https://hbr.org/2013/01/jeff-bezos-on-leading-for-the.

[12] Joseph H. Royer, "Milton S. Hershey The Candy Man," *Entrepreneur*, October 8, 2008, https://www.entrepreneur.com/article/197530.

[13] Eric Newcomer and Brad Stone, "The Fall of Travis Kalanick Was a Lot Weirder and Darker Than You Thought," January 18, 2018, https://www.bloomberg.com/news/features/2018-01-18/the-fall-of-travis-kalanick-was-a-lot-weirder-and-darker-than-you-thought.

[14] Newcomer and Stone.

[15] Eric Newcomer, "In Video, Uber's CEO Argues With a Driver Over Falling Fares," February 28, 2017, https://www.bloomberg.com/news/articles/2017-02-28/in-video-uber-ceo-argues-with-driver-over-falling-fares.

[16] Costas Pitas, "Uber CEO Tells London: I'm Sorry for the Mistakes We've Made," *Reuters*, September 25, 2017, https://www.reuters.com/article/us-uber-britain-cco-idUSKCN1C015W.

[17] Justin Bariso, "Uber's New CEO Just Sent an Amazing Email to Employees--and Taught a Major Lesson in Emotional Intelligence," Inc.com, September 23, 2017, https://www.inc.com/justin-bariso/ubers-new-ceo-just-sent-an-amazing-email-to-employees-taught-a-major-lesson-in-emotional-intelligence.html.

[18] Dara Khosrowshahi, "Uber's New Cultural Norms," LinkedIn, n.d., https://www.linkedin.com/pulse/ubers-new-cultural-norms-dara-khosrowshahi/.

Chapter 2

[1] Kerr, S (1975). On the folly of rewarding A, while hoping for B. *Academy of Management Journal, 18,* 769-783.

[2] Steve Kerr and Glenn Rifkin, *Reward Systems: Does Yours Measure Up?* (Harvard Business Press, 2008).

[3] Robert I. Sutton, "How Bosses Waste Their Employees' Time," The Wall Street Journal, August 12, 2018, https://www.dontwait.wsj.com/2018/Waste-Time.html.

[4] Sutton.

[5] Taleb, Skin in the Game.

[6] Kerr and Rifkin, *Reward Systems*.

[7] Bryce G. Hoffman, *American Icon: Alan Mulally and the Fight to Save Ford Motor Company* (Crown Business, 2013).

[8] Vivek Ramaswamy and Ken Banta, "This Pharma Company Stays Innovative by Doing Two Things," *Harvard Business Review*, March 14, 2017, https://hbr.org/2017/03/this-pharma-company-stays-innovative-by-doing-two-things.

[9] George Mandler, *The Structure of Value: Accounting for Taste* (Center for Human Information Processing, Department of Psychology, University of California, San Diego, 1981).

[10] Ming Hsu, Cédric Anen, and Steven R. Quartz, "The Right and the Good: Distributive Justice and Neural Encoding of Equity and Efficiency," *Science* 320, no. 5879 (2008): 1092–95.

[11] Bradley Kirkman et al., "Teamwork Works Best When Top Performers Are Rewarded," *Harvard Business Review*, March 14, 2016,

https://hbr.org/2016/03/teamwork-works-best-when-top-performers-are-rewarded.

[12] J. Greene and J. Baron, "Intuitions about Declining Marginal Utility," *Journal of Behavioral Decision Making* 14 (2001): 243–55.

[13] Daniel Kahneman, "Maps of Bounded Rationality: Psychology for Behavioral Economics," *American Economic Review* 93, no. 5 (December 2003): 1449–75, https://doi.org/10.1257/000282803322655392.

[14] TINYpulse, "Finance & Insurance Industry Employee Engagement Report | TINYpulse," accessed April 19, 2019, https://www.tinypulse.com/resources/finance-and-insurance-employee-engagement-report.

[15] Victor Lipman, "Employee Recognition: Cost-Free To Provide, Costly To Neglect," Forbes, accessed April 19, 2019, https://www.forbes.com/sites/victorlipman/2015/05/12/employee-recognition-cost-free-to-provide-costly-to-neglect/.

[16] Kerr, S (1975). On the folly of rewarding A, while hoping for B. *Academy of Management Journal, 18*, 769-783.

Chapter 3

[1] Irwin Kula and Craig Hatkoff, "Pope Francis: CEO and Epic Innovator," Forbes, November 12, 2014, https://www.forbes.com/sites/offwhitepapers/2014/11/12/pope-francis-secret-sauce-stop-pontificating/.

[2] Sylvia Poggioli, "With Vatican In Turmoil Over Abuse Allegations, Questions Remain About What Pope Knew," NPR, August 29, 2018, https://www.npr.org/2018/08/29/642680906/with-vatican-in-turmoil-over-abuse-allegations-questions-remain-about-what-pope.

[3] Jerry Useem, "How Corporations Become Evil," The Atlantic, December 21, 2015, https://www.theatlantic.com/magazine/archive/2016/01/what-was-volkswagen-thinking/419127/.

[4] Goldsmith, M. (2002). "The Six-Question Process." *Insights*. Available at www.marshallgoldsmith.com/articles/article.asp?a_id=87. Retrieved July 14, 2008.

[5] Kevin Webb, "Riot Games Suspends COO Scott Gelb for His Role in Company Bro Culture," Business Insider, December 14, 2018, https://www.businessinsider.com/riot-games-suspends-coo-scott-gelb-bro-culture-2018-12.

[6] Keith D. Markman and Philip E. Tetlock, "'I Couldn't Have Known': Accountability, Foreseeability and Counterfactual Denials of Responsibility," *British Journal of Social Psychology* 39, no. 3 (2000): 313–25, https://doi.org/10.1348/014466600164499.

[7] Lou Solomon, "Two-Thirds of Managers Are Uncomfortable Communicating with Employees," *Harvard Business Review*, March 9, 2016, https://hbr.org/2016/03/two-thirds-of-managers-are-uncomfortable-communicating-with-employees.

[8] Peter R. Neumann, "Negotiating With Terrorists," September 15, 2015, https://www.foreignaffairs.com/articles/2007-01-01/negotiating-terrorists.

[9] "Trump Handshake Not Innocent - Macron," May 28, 2017, sec. Europe, https://www.bbc.com/news/world-europe-40077241.

[10] George L. Kelling Wilson James Q., "Broken Windows," The Atlantic, March 1, 1982, https://www.theatlantic.com/magazine/archive/1982/03/broken-windows/304465/.

[11] John M. Darley and C. Daniel Baston, "'From Jerusalem to Jericho': A Study of Situational and Dispositional Variables in Helping Behavior," *Journal of Personality and Social Psychology* 100:27 (July 1973), http://dx.doi.org/10.1037/h0034449.

[12] Nassim Nicholas Taleb, Skin in the Game, Incerto (Random House, 2018), https://en.wikipedia.org/w/index.php?title=Skin_in_the_Game_(book)&oldid=880234475.

[13] Taleb.

[14] Geoff Ziezulewicz, "'I Now Hate My Ship': Surveys Reveal Disastrous Morale on Cruiser Shiloh," Navy Times, October 10, 2017, https://www.navytimes.com/news/your-navy/2017/10/09/i-now-hate-my-ship-surveys-reveal-disastrous-morale-on-cruiser-shiloh/.

[15] Lila MacLellan, "The Ultimate Case against Using Shame as a Management Tactic," Quartz, July 30, 2017, https://qz.com/1039957/the-ultimate-case-against-using-shame-as-a-management-tactic/.

[16] Gary P. Pisano, "The Hard Truth About Innovative Cultures," *Harvard Business Review*, January 1, 2019, https://hbr.org/2019/01/the-hard-truth-about-innovative-cultures.

Chapter 4

[1] Gene Marks, "The Leadership Lesson I Learned Waiting for My Flight to Crash Land," Entrepreneur, September 28, 2017, https://www.entrepreneur.com/article/300947.

[2] Robert J. Anderson and William A. Adams, *Scaling Leadership: Building Organizational Capability and Capacity to Create Outcomes That Matter Most* (John Wiley & Sons, 2019).

[3] Amy C. Edmondson, "How Fearless Organizations Succeed," strategy+business, November 14, 2018, https://www.strategy-business.com/article/How-Fearless-Organizations-Succeed?gko=63131.

[4] Julia Rozovsky, "Re:Work - The Five Keys to a Successful Google Team," November 17, 2015, https://rework.withgoogle.com/blog/five-keys-to-a-successful-google-team/.

[5] Laura Delizonna, "High-Performing Teams Need Psychological Safety. Here's How to Create It," *Harvard Business Review*, August 24, 2017, https://hbr.org/2017/08/high-performing-teams-need-psychological-safety-heres-how-to-create-it.

[6] Lauren Ingram, "Lesbian Woman Walked down the Aisle by Her Boss," Mail Online, March 9, 2017, http://www.dailymail.co.uk/~/article-4295316/index.html.

[7] Joseph Grenny, "How to Raise Sensitive Issues During a Virtual Meeting," *Harvard Business Review*, March 14, 2017, https://hbr.org/2017/03/how-to-raise-sensitive-issues-during-a-virtual-meeting.

[8] Naomi I. Eisenberger, Matthew D. Lieberman, and Kipling D. Williams, "Does Rejection Hurt? An FMRI Study of Social Exclusion," *Science (New York, N.Y.)* 302, no. 5643 (October 10, 2003): 290–92, https://doi.org/10.1126/science.1089134.

[9] Nassim Nicholas Taleb, Skin in the Game (p. 170), Incerto (Random House, 2018), https://en.wikipedia.org/w/index.php?title=Skin_in_the_Game_(book)&oldid=8 80234475.

[10] Justin Bariso, "This Email From Elon Musk to Tesla Employees Describes What Great Communication Looks Like," Inc.com, August 30, 2017, https://www.inc.com/justin-bariso/this-email-from-elon-musk-to-tesla-employees-descr.html.

[11] James Marshall, "The 6 Best and Worst CEOs of 2017 and What You Can Learn from Them | Aventr," September 7, 2017, https://www.aventr.com/blog/the-6-best-and-worse-ceos-of-2017-and-what-you-can-learn-from-them.

[12] John Gottman, *Why Marriages Succeed or Fail* (A&C Black, 2012).

[13] Richard Conniff, *The Ape in the Corner Office: Understanding the Workplace Beast in All of Us* (Crown Publishing Group, 2005).

[14] Sandra Aamodt and Sam Wang, *Welcome to Your Brain: Why You Lose Your Car Keys but Never Forget How to Drive and Other Puzzles of Everyday Life* (Bloomsbury Publishing USA, 2010).

[15] Malcolm Gladwell, "Here's Why," April 3, 2006, https://www.newyorker.com/magazine/2006/04/10/heres-why.

[16] David Grant et al., *The SAGE Handbook of Organizational Discourse* (SAGE, 2004).

[17] Karl E. Weick and Kathleen M. Sutcliffe, *Managing the Unexpected: Resilient Performance in an Age of Uncertainty* (John Wiley & Sons, 2011).

[18] Gillian Fournier, "Locus of Control," Encyclopedia of Psychology, June 17, 2016, https://psychcentral.com/encyclopedia/locus-of-control/.

[19] Bruce Daisley, "How Laughter Makes You a Better Worker," April 4, 2018, http://www.bbc.com/capital/story/20180404-how-laughter-makes-you-a-better-worker.

[20] Rebecca Bernstein, "Interesting Psychological Phenomena: The Pratfall Effect," BUonline, June 26, 2017, https://online.brescia.edu/psychology-news/pratfall-effect/.

[21] Christian Cotroneo, "How One Woman Found Her Calling in Failure," MNN - Mother Nature Network, February 5, 2018, https://www.mnn.com/money/sustainable-business-practices/stories/failure-institute-gasca.

[22] James Watkins, "This Woman Started a Global Movement Based on Her Failure," OZY, May 5, 2017, http://www.ozy.com/rising-stars/the-worldwide-success-of-the-queen-of-failure/75675.

Chapter 5

[1] Martin Greenberger, Johns Hopkins University, and Brookings Institution, *Computers, Communications, and the Public Interest* (Johns Hopkins Press, 1971).

[2] "How Often Do You Check Your Phone? Most Do It 110 Times a DAY," Mail Online, October 8, 2013, https://www.dailymail.co.uk/sciencetech/article-

2449632/How-check-phone-The-average-person-does-110-times-DAY-6-seconds-evening.html.

[3] Christopher Booker, *The Seven Basic Plots: Why We Tell Stories* (Bloomsbury Publishing, 2005).

[4] Patti Waldmeir, "Mayor Mike Duggan: How I Am Halting Detroit's Decline," Financial Times, January 7, 2018, https://www.ft.com/content/735f82c2-e703-11e7-8b99-0191e45377ec.

[5] Teresa Amabile and Steven J. Kramer, "The Power of Small Wins," *Harvard Business Review*, May 1, 2011, https://hbr.org/2011/05/the-power-of-small-wins.

[6] Carmine Gallo, "What Richard Branson and Phil Knight Teach Us About Brand Storytelling," Inc.com, June 27, 2017, https://www.inc.com/carmine-gallo/your-company-needs-a-chief-storyteller-like-richard-branson-and-phil-knight.html.

[7] Jim VandeHei, "The Axios Way: How You Do It," Axios, accessed April 19, 2019, https://www.axios.com/the-axios-way-how-you-do-it-1513304963-a1383ac1-a4a0-413e-9338-21d2874ba95d.html.

[8] T. J. Larkin and Sandar Larkin, *Communicating Change: Winning Employee Support for New Business Goals* (McGraw Hill Professional, 1994).

Chapter 6
[1] Barbara Starr Correspondent CNN Pentagon, "Air Force Says Boeing Has 'severe situation' after Trash Found on Refueling Planes," CNN, n.d., https://www.cnn.com/2019/03/14/politics/air-force-boeing-refueling-plane/index.html.

Made in the USA
Columbia, SC
29 January 2020